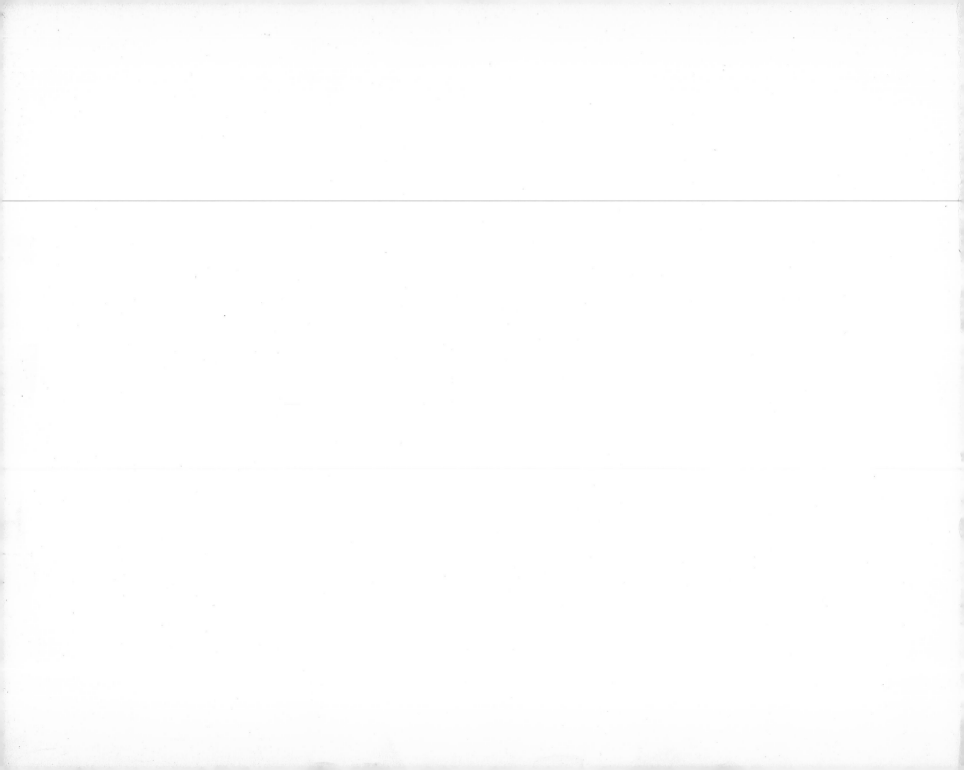

Sailing for America's Cup

by
EVERETT B. MORRIS

photographs by
MORRIS ROSENFELD

foreword by
EMIL MOSBACHER, JR.

SAILING

FOR AMERICA'S CUP

Harper & Row, Publishers

New York, Evanston, and London

SAILING FOR AMERICA'S CUP

LIBRARY OF CONGRESS CATALOG CARD NUMBER: 63–17718

FIRST EDITION

CONTENTS

FOREWORD
by Emil Mosbacher, Jr.   vii

THE CUP
Tradition's Symbol   3

THE SKIPPER
The Man Who Must Have Everything   15

THE CREW
Supporting Cast for the Star   45

DEVELOPING THE TEAM
How a Winning Combination Is Put Together   67

MATCH RACE TACTICS
Where Mistakes Hurt Most   93

TO THE LADIES
Their Role in Cup Competition   135

THE DEEDS OF GIFT
A Study in Progressive Sportsmanship   149
Comparison of Class J and 12-Meter Boats   169

A LOOK AHEAD
The Line Forms to the Right   175

A LOOK BACK
Cup Competition in Retrospect   197

APPENDICES
The America's Cup Record   202
Yachts' Vital Statistics   206
Defender and Challenger Owners   208
Contenders Eliminated in Trials to Select Defenders   210

GLOSSARY   214

As one who has been fortunate enough to have successfully survived a defense of the "Auld Mug" I still view the subject with reverence and awe. This wonderful tradition of international sailing competition—a reminder of our country's early and great seafaring tradition—is, I believe, to be cherished and treasured. Winning is important, vitally so. But more important is that we continue to attempt the defense—yes, and recapture the Cup when it becomes necessary, in the spirit of hard, keen, sporting competition, giving and taking with the world's best sailors.

The painfully careful planning, the blistering hard work, the brain-wracking ingenuity of designer and sailmaker have here been recounted far more completely than ever before for this age of modern 12-Meter sailing.

This era began in 1958 when we saw, for the first time, the Cup defended in 12-Meters and when, too, crews were mainly native-born amateurs competing for the love of the sport. Also for the first time there was a mass invasion of "big boats" by small-boat sailors. In a few months a sport was revolutionized. What was lost in the passing of the majestic J boats was, at least partly, compensated for by exciting new racing techniques and tactics.

There have been a number of excellent articles on various phases of the tradition and history of this distinctive sports trophy: the evolution and revolution, the training and tactics, the conditioning of men and machine, the happiness and heartbreak, connected with this endeavor. I don't believe, though, that there has been a more

FOREWORD

understandingly precise and detailed account ever of this great experience.

Ev Morris, naval captain, sports writer extraordinaire, former president of Junior Yacht Racing Association of Long Island Sound, former president of the Basketball Writers Association, coach, Race Committeeman, has salt spray in his blood and the seafaring lore of the rugged New England coast as his heritage. Fortunately for us he has devoted most of his energy to yachting. No one less richly endowed than this articulate reporter and historian could capture and relate as accurately in the sailorman's colorful vernacular the spirit and the substance that make the America's Cup.

I have enjoyed immensely reliving these happy, exciting memories with Ev and shall always keep this book as a cheerful reminder of a lifetime dream come true.

Emil Mosbacher, Jr.

THE CUP

Tradition's Symbol

The reverent speak of it only as the Cup, a misnomer sanctioned by time and custom. The prize, named for the rakish Yankee racing schooner which brought it home in triumph from England in the middle of the nineteenth century, is not a cup at all.

It is a tall and rather grotesque sterling pitcher that lacks even the saving grace of utility—its bottom long ago was pierced for the bolt which moors it to a heavy oaken table in the New York Yacht Club's trophy room. In this yachting shrine, the America's Cup holds only the misty fabric of men's dreams, a gossamer powdered with the iridescent dust of history and sea romance. No festive wine pours from its spout at victory rites—even those who have won it may only look upon the receptacle and speculate as to its original capacity.

The old ewer would win few if any awards today for artistic excellence. It would fetch little in the used silver market. But lack of neither esthetic appeal nor material value has prevented the America's Cup from becoming a priceless symbol of international sailing supremacy.

On no other sporting prize has so much gold, technical virtuosity, brain power, and brawn been expended since the first bloodless sea battle was fought for its possession off the English coast. No other marine laurel surpasses the America's Cup in the richness of the tradition with which it has been endowed by generations of contentious, hard-driving seamen. Few other trophies come to mind whose winning or losing stirs so much emotion in a people, involves so heavily the pride and prestige of nations.

Perhaps the variance between shape and name in some way is linked to the contradictions, the contrasts which have marked the sporadic and uniformly unsuccessful attempts to dislodge the trophy. New York has been its home ever since Commodore John Cox Stevens and his associates in *America* earned it and Queen Victoria's personally delivered congratulations by outsailing the Royal Yacht Squadron's finest in a race around the Isle of Wight on August 22, 1851.

Every flute, curlicue, plaquette, and whorl with which the baroque surface of the pitcher is so abundantly adorned is matched in Cup history by shining achievements and profound disappointments; tolerant understanding and childish displays of bad manners and sulphurous temper; generous sportsmanship and niggling parochialism; some instances of commercial motivation and more of unassailable Corinthianism; exciting racing and dismal mismatches.

Just as the polished curves of the Cup reflect the light filtering through the thick glass case that shelters it from city grime and the corrosive touch of curious fingers, so do the variants of human behavior and accomplishment mirror the living side of what has come to be the treasure at the end of yachting's rainbow. Human frailties and strengths have given it life.

3

Men design, build, and race vessels to represent their countries in quest of a victory symbolizing pre-eminence among those peoples whose sons still go down to the sea in sailing ships. Men give of their fortunes, their genius, their physical strength in quest and defense of this ornate souvenir of the occasion which signaled the emergence of the United States as a yachting power.

Yachts have changed in a hundred years. So have those who man them and administer their racing. While Cup defenders and challengers have shrunk in the face of swelling taxes, appreciation of what the Cup represents has grown as has sailing officialdom's approach to sportsmanship.

Gone are the large crews of professional seamen who heaved and hauled on the heavy cordage and manhandled the cumbersome gear of the *Madeleine*s, the *Genesta*s, the *Valkyrie*s, the *Vigilant*s and their kind. With them have disappeared the little men, the club officials whose creed was "never give the challenger a break," and the frustrated, short-sport losers whose fulminations and irresponsible accusations were more suited to a back alley dice game than to a sport supposedly engaged in by gentlemen.

The rugged seamen who worked in Cup yachts for wages and found—if fortunate in their choice of employer—a share of the prize money have yielded to eager, skilled amateurs who forsake business, pleasure, and sometimes family to strive for a niche in sailing's hall of fame and the satisfaction which comes to those who have manned an America's Cup defender.

Happily, those who spent their time devising ways and means of obstructing challengers have been long gone from the committees in whose hands rest America's Cup affairs. Their successors are sailing on the opposite tack, doing everything within reason—and sometimes, it has seemed, a little more—to assist and encourage sailors who have come from overseas in quest of what some romanticists call "the Golden Fleece of yachting."

So a competition once almost wholly professional in personnel and spirit has become the quintessence of amateurism in both elements. Economics played an important part in the evolution; no one in yachting today could afford the huge sail carriers of the late nineteenth and early twentieth centuries, and the enormous crews of paid hands required to man them.

It is a long step—and few will argue that it is not in the right direction—from the 124-foot *Vigilant* of 1893 whose seventy seamen wrestled with more than a quarter-acre of canvas to a 69-foot sloop of the International 12-Meter Class so efficient in hull, sail plan, deck layout, and equipment that only eleven men are permitted, or for that matter needed, in the crew. And that includes the lot—skipper, navigator, afterguard, and deckhands.

There is provision in the rules for employment of three professionals in a 12-Meter crew at the owner's option, but neither victorious *Weatherly* nor her Australian rival, *Gretel,* had even one aboard in their stirring 1962 match. *Columbia* and *Sceptre,* which ushered in the 12-Meter era of America's Cup history in 1958, had some professionals in their complements and there were others working in the Twelves seeking nomination as the New York Yacht Club defender in the trials sailed that summer.

There was good reason for professionals in the first 12-Meters built for the Cup defense. In the United States at that time there were very few amateur sailors with experience in Twelves or any other racing machine of comparable size and complexity. There was real need for the guidance which such first-class sailing masters as Fred Lawton of *Columbia* and Willie Carstens of *Vim* could and did provide. These highly skilled, practical seamen, though, were much closer to their amateur shipmates in dedication and competitive zeal than were the numerous, bell-bottom trousered sailors of *Reliance,* for example. A good deal of the Lawton-Carstens pride of craft, deeply rooted love of sailing, self-confidence, and skills acquired in a different

⚓

The Cup, worth 100 guineas when the Royal Yacht Squadron offered it for a race around the Island of Wight on August 22, 1851, is now a trophy without price and the symbol of international sailing supremacy. It is bolted to a table in the trophy room of the New York Yacht Club.

5

America *from a drawing in the* London Illustrated News *of August 30, 1851. It shows the schooner for which the Cup is named in her original rig—heavily raked spars, main gaff topsail, and baldheaded foremast.*

America *after her rig had been modernized under the ownership of General Benjamin F. Butler of Boston and she returned to racing. The General bought her at auction from the U.S. Navy in 1873 after she had served in the Civil War, first as a Confederate blockade runner and later as a Union warship, before becoming a Naval Academy schoolship. America sailed her last yacht race in 1901.*

Vanitie (1920). *Beaten by* Resolute *in the trials preceding the defense against* Shamrock IV, *beautiful* Vanitie *came back ten years later to serve as a trial horse for the four new J boats contesting the honor of meeting* Shamrock V. *She is shown here smoking along with lifted sheets at an impressive rate of knots, her cluttered foredeck—bitts, capstan, skylight, and toe-stubbers—a contrast to the clean, functional foredecks of the Twelves.*

Reliance (1903) *running before the wind under all of her 16,159 square feet of canvas plus that in her tall, single luff spinnaker, the pole for which was about as long as the mast of a modern 12-Meter sloop. She was the largest yacht overall (143 feet) ever to race for the Cup and the last of the huge sail-carrying skimming dishes. A rules change after her easy victory of Shamrock III rang down the curtain on her type—flat, light displacement scows with what amounted to fin keels.*

Vigilant (1893) *first of the five Nat Herreshoff-designed and built Cup defenders. She was the first with a spoon bow and the first to be plated with Tobin bronze below the waterline. Her upper strakes were steel. Vigilant's centerboard, 16 feet long with 10 feet across, was bronze plated and filled with concrete to a weight of 7750 pounds.*

and difficult school rubbed off on appreciative Corinthian associates.

Consequently, after two America's Cup matches and the adequate if not abundant racing which spiced the summers between, the United States has a reasonably large pool of yachtsmen experienced in 12-Meter yachts. This goes for helmsmen as well as winch grinders and foredeck hands.

Philip L. Rhodes, a naval architect of great experience and versatility, as well as some modesty (he calls it realism), has often revealed his own scale of values of the elements which go into the making of a successful Cup candidate, or, for that matter, of any other racing yacht. He ranks them in this order of importance: (1) crew, including helmsman; (2) sails; (3) hull, including rig. Sometimes he adds a fourth factor, although he insists that it should not be necessary to do so ("It should be understood")—a good owner. By Rhodes's definition, a good owner is one with a quick fountain pen and no desire to meddle in the operation.

Weatherly, which was designed by Rhodes in 1958 and became a winner four years later after failing the first time around, had all of the required components and in the right proportions. Just what these proportions are is a matter of opinion, but Rhodes for one believes that when you get up into the big leagues the differences between factors become less, the gaps between them narrower. The blending of the basic ingredients into a successful whole is so smooth as to blur distinctions: unity and balance have been achieved between men and materials.

When this occurs, the odds are heavily in favor of one man being responsible for the effective amalgam. Look for him in the cockpit, behind the wheel. No matter how fast the hull, how fine her equipment, how skillful and efficient the crew, a yacht striving for the honor of defending the Cup cannot attain her goal unless her command is vested in a skipper of exceptional ability.

The competition leading up to selection as defender is extremely arduous and testing in so many ways. Ability far beyond the normal range is required of the yachtsman whose task it becomes to take a boat through a summer-long grind of sail setting and changing, tacking and jibing, reaching, running, and slogging to windward in fair weather and foul against opponents quick to capitalize on the slightest mistake in tactics or technique.

THE SKIPPER

The Man Who Must Have Everything

.

If the crew is the most important element in the making of a winning racing vessel, it follows that the skipper is the most important member of the team. For he is its quarterback, its field strategist and tactician, its brains and heart.

Hugh Somerville, the knowing observer of the British yachting scene who was *Sceptre*'s Boswell, insists that the skipper must be a dictator as well.

"Boats and crews do not respond to committees or democracy," he says in his biography of the 1958 challenger, apropos her difficulties. "They require dictatorial command. It requires considerable skill to find the right dictator."

Few men in any sport carry the responsibilities borne by an America's Cup skipper; so much is expected, so much demanded of him ashore as well as afloat. The miracle is that we always have had in the United States the necessary paragon with the dash of genius it takes to do the job. This is one of the primary reasons why, in the 113 years which have slipped over the horizon since Captain Dick Brown steered *America* to her conquest of England's finest, the trophy she won has never left these shores.

When the time comes to select the man on whom he must pin his hopes for success in a Cup venture, what does an owner or manager of an ownership syndicate look for in a skipper?

Tastes vary with owners and syndicates. Personalities and prejudices become involved as well as different standards for measuring a commander's worth. It is a fact, however, that all of our great Cup defender skippers, professional and amateur, possessed to an unusual degree the following qualities:

1. A solid racing background; wide range of experience.
2. Well-developed tactical and technical skills.
3. Organizing and administrative ability.
4. Physical endurance and resilience.
5. Strong competitive drive.
6. Whole-souled dedication to the task.
7. Leadership.

Charley Barr, the little Scotsman who turned back the first three of Sir Thomas Lipton's *Shamrock*s, and who was the sharpest of the professional captains, was geared to these requirements. So was Commodore Harold S. Vanderbilt, who equaled in the short-lived J boat era Barr's feat of sailing three successive Cup defenders. So also was Emil (Bus) Mosbacher, Jr., whose touch brought *Weatherly* to life for the eighteenth defense and performed such prodigies in *Vim* four years earlier.

They had other characteristics in common, these three. All were dictators in the Somervillian sense; they exercised full command, made all decisions. They were firm disciplinarians, hard drillmasters, perfectionists. They settled, like the seamen they were, for nothing short of the best—

best in gear, best in sails, and best in effort from their shipmates. And they demanded no more of their shipmates than they gave themselves, less in fact, as they strove endlessly to make their boats sail faster.

Vanderbilt wrote after his conquest of *Shamrock V* in 1930: "A large sailing yacht . . . is never finished, never perfect." Mosbacher read, and never forgot, that statement and others of significance in Vanderbilt's books, well-thumbed copies of which are in his library. There is not much doubt that the yachtsman-author who ruled the Cup waves with *Enterprise, Rainbow,* and *Ranger* was Mosbacher's inspiration, and even less question that, unconsciously perhaps, the young man who was to be the hero of 1958 and 1962 adopted and practiced the doctrine of perfectionism which Vanderbilt preached in the 1930's— there are just too many similarities in the way they do things for coincidence.

In their authoritative history of Cup competition, *The America's Cup Races,* the late Herbert L. Stone and his *Yachting* magazine colleague, William H. Taylor, had this to say of Vanderbilt after *Enterprise* had been selected to defend against *Shamrock V:*

He was an excellent helmsman, tactician, strategist and judge of boats and weather . . . he had what a big-yacht skipper needs: the ability to pick good men to sail with him, to delegate responsibility to them and benefit by trusting their advice and actions, and he was a master organizer of racing crews.

What was true of Vanderbilt in the thirties is true of Mosbacher now. The tremendous fight he put up in 1958 with the then nineteen-year-old *Vim* against the new *Columbia,* and the renaissance of *Weatherly* under his painstaking guidance four years later is proof that he has those qualities.

Yet his preparation for the role of Cup defender skipper was a good deal different from that of the tall commodore who became one of his sincerest admirers. Handling 165-ton, 135-foot-long Class J sloops with 165-foot masts came relatively easy to Vanderbilt. He had always owned and raced large yachts; big, high-hatted racing schooners like *Vagrant,* tall, long-legged Class M sloops like *Prestige.* Mosbacher built the foundation for his career in the 12-Meter Class yachts now in America's Cup vogue by competing on Long Island Sound in one-design class sloops of 23 to 33 feet over-all length, steering International 6-Meter boats abroad and, finally, as helmsman and watch officer in offshore cruising racers.

Yachting was a big-boat sport when Harold Sterling Vanderbilt was moving along his course to yachting im-

⚓

Deck scene on Endeavour (1934) *taken shortly after she had crossed the line in one of her two victories over* Rainbow. *T.O.M. Sopwith, at the wheel, and Mrs. Sopwith, the skipper's wife, standing in the hatch.*

16

mortality. A stock market crash and the ensuing economic depression radically altered a yachtsman's way of life before Mosbacher graduated from the junior ranks. Yacht sizes were reduced to match declining bank accounts, but a liberal education in the sailing arts was still available to anyone willing to work for it, who had the ability to learn from experience and observation and profit from the advice and mistakes of others. Mosbacher was that kind of a boy when he first stood out from his junior racing contemporaries and he had not changed in this respect at forty when he was steering *Weatherly* safely around the rocks and shoals and tide rips that encumber the approaches to Cup fame.

Whereas Vanderbilt's view of the development of a winning Class J sloop was that of a studious, inquiring man of science, Mosbacher's continuous search for ways and means to make *Weatherly* go faster reflected the practicality of his small-boat background and the seamanship of his deep-water experience. Although different in this regard, they shared the belief that there is always something of value to be learned by listening to those whose words they respect and from experimenting with promising ideas.

Vanderbilt's real appreciation of complex engineering principles surprised and delighted W. Starling Burgess, the versatile and volatile genius who designed the commodore's Cup yachts and conceived most of the advanced

gadgets with which they were equipped. Mosbacher's passion for weight- and labor-saving measures without sacrifice of seaworthiness and efficiency made Eddie Bainbridge, *Weatherly*'s devoted equivalent of a port engineer and consulting naval architect, the busiest man in Newport in 1962. And this does not exclude Alan Payne, who not only designed *Gretel* but did everything else for her except sweep and wash down before, during, and after her exciting effort to give Australia a winner in that country's first Cup venture.

Enterprise was referred to frequently, and not without reason, as a "floating machine shop." Proper tension for standing rigging and backstays was determined by instruments. She carried the first duralumin mast in a Cup yacht, a slender spar weighing only 4,000 pounds. She had a flat-topped "Park Avenue" boom whose cross streets were transverse sail slides that allowed the foot of her mainsail to be set in the proper aerodynamic curve for a variety of wind conditions. Below decks she had batteries of winches and reels to which all running gear and back-

⚓

The British are not always formal, witness Tom Sopwith in shirtsleeves, white flannel bags (appropriate English name for these voluminous trousers) and yachting cap, looking out to weather as he drives the first Endeavour *to windward in gentle air and smooth sea.*

18

stays were led. Eight of Vanderbilt's sailors, nicknamed the "black gang" by their shipmates, never saw a race. Their battle stations were inside the cavernous hull and it was their duty to man the multiple Vanderbilt-Burgess mechanical aids to sail and rig adjustment. *Enterprise* was an engineer's heaven.

Weatherly was not nearly that mechanized—rules revisions since *Enterprise*'s day have changed many things—and all of her crew worked topside except, of course, the navigator, who necessarily had to go below now and then to do his plotting and fiddle with the dials on his time-distance computer. *Weatherly*'s problem was weight, or, to be strictly accurate, the distribution thereof. Through a miscalculation, *Weatherly*'s keel was cast more than half a ton light, a circumstance which made her tender in wind of any real strength. She was written off in 1958 as strictly a light-weather boat.

When Mosbacher took over before the 1962 campaign, he set ruthlessly about the job of transforming excess above-the-waterline weight into stability-increasing ballast. He shifted all of the halyard and lift winches and cleats from the mast to *Weatherly*'s deck, thus lowering this weight several feet. It did not weigh much, but he junked a metal masthead wind-direction indicator, because for every pound up there—ninety feet aloft—ten would be needed in ballast to neutralize its heeling effect. He removed every expendable fitting from cabin and cockpit,

even the pipe rack installed by his predecessor—Mosbacher doesn't smoke and the rack represented wasted ounces. Off came the footrails running along the edges of the deck; every sliver of wood topside and below which was not performing some vital function went overside.

So did one of the yacht's large, heavy-duty winches. To compensate for the loss of this item of deck machinery, Mosbacher devised new routines for every evolution in which the discarded winch might have been used. This was the work of the practical perfectionist, a racing man acting on his own experience and the advice of those who had his confidence. It paid off handsomely. *Weatherly* was stiffer and faster than ever she had been, and her crew readily adjusted to the new sail-handling techniques despite the added burden on their muscles and timing.

Selecting a skipper to take charge of a Cup defense candidate is a task as varied as the personalities of the men engaged in it and the times in which they lived.

⚓

Weatherly, *hard on the wind on the port tack. As* Weatherly *approaches the Narragansett shore in one of her trial races, helmsman Mosbacher looks back over his shoulder at the opposition, presumably, while navigator Dick Matthews (in dark shirt) looks the other way to take a bearing on whatever obstacle* Weatherly *will have to clear after going around onto the starboard tack.*

Until the *Resolute-Shamrock IV* match of 1920, when amateurs commanded both defender and challenger for the first time (Charles Francis Adams, the American yacht; William P. Burton—later Sir William—the British hopeful) it was largely a matter of picking the best available professional sailing master and letting him get on with the job. Competent, experienced amateurs for big-boat command were not to be had, simply because in those days owners hired captains to race their boats much as they retained jockeys to ride their race horses.

Ten years after the professional monopoly on Cup yacht command was broken, the amateur pattern became firmly rooted. Every one of the four Cup defense candidates in 1930 had a sportsman skipper, and in no case did the owning syndicate have to go outside of its own ranks to find him. He was a member of the organization which raised the funds to build a yacht, commissioned a designer to draw the plans, contracted with Herreshoff or Lawley to construct her, and then paid the impressive bills for the summer-long campaign.

Professional captains and mates had nothing to do with the command or tactical departments. Their job was to hire, train, discipline, and direct the work of the score or more of Down-East and Scandinavian paid hands who made up the crew; the orders came from aft, where everyone was an amateur yachtsman of established stature. Decisions as to which sails to set or strike, whether to trim or ease, whether to tack or jibe were made by Charles Francis Adams, George Nichols, John S. Lawrence, George M. Pynchon, Frank C. Paine and their kind.

Enterprise was a perfect example of the new disposition of authority. Commodore Vanderbilt, a large shareholder in the syndicate, was in charge afloat. The syndicate manager, Winthrop W. Aldrich, took the navigator's billet. The other members of the afterguard, or "brain trust," were Burgess, the engineering wizard who designed the yacht, its ingenious components and gear; the incomparable C. Sherman Hoyt, who had few peers anywhere as helmsman or sail trimmer, and Charles F. (Bubbles) Havemeyer, a quiet, extremely efficient and astute sailor of wide experience. Either Hoyt or Havemeyer could do a first-rate job at the helm whenever Vanderbilt asked to be spelled, and both had such a thorough knowledge of racing techniques and tactics that they were invaluable aides and advisors to the skipper.

Captain George Monsell, the Greenport, Long Island, master mariner, who had been with Vanderbilt since the early days of the schooner *Vagrant* and was captain of his motor yacht *Vara*, and Harry Klefve, his mate, put the crew together, instructed the men in their duties, kept them in line and happy, and, under Vanderbilt's eye, drilled them until they could execute assignments with smoothness and precision regardless of weather and competitive pressure.

Before America's Cup rivalry was revived in 1958 after a twenty-one-year lapse, the rules were changed to make it possible for yachts as small as International 12-Meter Class sloops to race for the historic silver ewer. For all practical purposes this downward revision in size of eligible yachts rang the death knell of the professional deckhand and permanently relegated professional captains to the duties of boatswain or maintenance officer.

When three new Twelves were built in 1958 to race against the supposedly outmoded *Vim* for the right to meet the British challenger, *Sceptre*, two of the four yachts were commanded by skippers appointed by non-racing owners, one was run by the owner himself, with his two sons as helmsmen, and the other by a syndicate member.

The 12-Meter complements more than reversed the J boat ratio of twenty-five paid hands to five amateurs. Out of crews limited by rule to eleven men, including the helmsman, *Vim* had three professionals, *Columbia* two, *Weatherly* and *Easterner* one each. Of the salaried sailors only two were prominent in the proceedings. Willie Carstens, a topnotch pro captain, was a key man in the *Vim* organization and had much to do with educating his shipmates in the peculiarities of a Twelve. Captain Fred Lawton, a wartime naval officer and Vanderbilt's sailing master in *Vim* when the commodore was leading the British Twelves a merry chase in their own waters in 1939, played an important role in the development of *Columbia* into a winner.

The summer of 1958 was significant in another respect.

It produced a family boat as a serious candidate for the defender's berth. This was *Easterner*, owned by Boston banker Chandler Hovey, who had been a member of *Yankee*'s syndicate and afterguard in 1930 and 1934, owned *Weetamoe* in 1936 and *Rainbow* a year later. He had made a practice of sailing his many racing boats with his two sons, Chandler (Bus), Jr., and Charles, and his daughter, Sis. At seventy-eight years of age he saw no reason to change this policy merely because he had decided to make another attempt to win the Cup defense trials.

As a matter of fact, he elaborated on it. Bus and Charley steered *Easterner*; Sis handled a cockpit job; her husband, Wells Morss, from another old Boston sailing family, was navigator; and in the deck gang there was always a Hovey grandchild or two.

Not until shortly before the final trials did Commodore Hovey take a leaf from his opponents' books and import crack amateur talent, cutting down on family participation. It was too late then. *Easterner* was eliminated with *Weatherly* early in the proceedings and ended the season without a victory. The blame could not be laid entirely on the family doorstep—the Hoveys need no apologists for their sailing ability—but *Easterner* was launched long after the other new Twelves and consequently was always a cable's length astern of her rivals in development.

The other Twelves were unencumbered by family sentiment. True, John N. (Captain Jack) Matthews shipped

Charles Francis Adams, *a legendary figure in New England sailing, was the first amateur helmsman to command a Cup defender. He sailed* Resolute *to victory over Sir Thomas Lipton's* Shamrock IV *in 1920 when she too was sailed by a Corinthian, Sir William Burton.*

Sir Thomas Lipton challenged for what he called "the auld mug" so often—five times—that many Americans came to call it "the Lipton Cup," even though he never won it. His amiability, fine sportsmanship, and keen sense of public relations made him extremely popular in the United States and did much to dispel the bad taste left by his predecessor as a challenger, the controversial Lord Dunraven.

Captain Charley Barr, a truly canny little Scottish sailing master, was three times skipper of an America's Cup defender, three times a conqueror of Shamrocks. He steered Columbia *in 1899 and 1901 against* Shamrock I *and* II, *and commanded the huge* Reliance *in 1903 when she widely outsailed* Shamrock III. *Captain Barr was the last and the best of the professionals who sailed our defenders.*

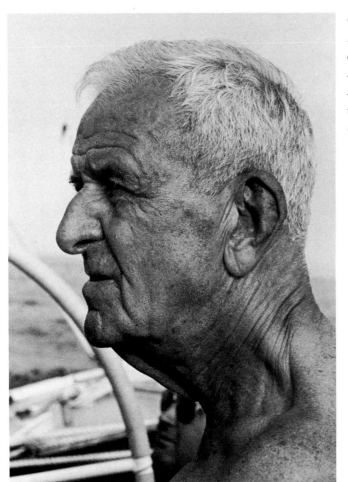

Chandler Hovey, today's link with the grand old days of Marblehead yachting, has known as many America's Cup disappointments as Sir Thomas Lipton, but from the other side of the competition. He was a member of the Yankee syndicate in 1930, and again in 1934. He owned Rainbow when she raced Ranger in 1937, and he tried twice more for the defense assignment in 1958 and 1962 with Easterner.

Briggs S. Cunningham, a first-rate racing skipper since his undergraduate days at Yale, brought great experience and competitive spirit to his assignment as Columbia's commander when she so easily defeated Britain's Sceptre in the first 12-Meter match for the Cup in 1958.

C. Sherman Hoyt, naval architect, bon vivant, and racing helmsman with few peers, was a key member of Commodore Vanderbilt's afterguard in Enterprise and Rainbow.

William Sellers Cox is new to big-boat racing, but the skipper of the Aurora syndicate's candidate for Cup defense honors in 1964 has a brilliant record as a helmsman and tactician dating back to 1930 when he won the Sears Bowl and national junior sailing championship for the Vineyard Haven Yacht Club.

two of his sons, Richard and Donald, in *Vim*'s crew of combat-seasoned hands, but when the time came to make a decision that would help his yacht's cause, he did not let parental ties hobble his judgment.

Columbia's skipper was Briggs S. Cunningham, a real competitor, whose extensive experience in the United States and abroad included sailing his father-in-law's 12-Meter *Nyala* in the mid-thirties, when Long Island Sound boasted a small but highly competitive fleet of the boats which later were to be elevated to America's Cup status. Arthur Knapp, Jr., was in charge of *Weatherly*. His yachting background spread from Frostbite dinghies to J boats (he had been in *Ranger*'s afterguard in 1937), through everything from Stars to ocean-racing yachts.

⚓

A formal portrait of Commodore Harold S. Vanderbilt at the wheel of Rainbow *(1934) in yachting cap and jacket, white flannels and shoes. The sailor leaning against the mainsheet in the background is not impressed.*

⚓

The Shields family triumvirate which campaigned Columbia *in 1962. Cornelius (Glit) Shields, Jr., at the helm; his father, Corny, Sr., (left) and uncle, Paul, Columbia's owner (right).*

28

Cunningham was a principal with Henry Sears, his navigator, in the *Columbia* syndicate. It was Sears, incidentally, who persuaded the British, when he was New York Yacht Club commodore in 1956, to agree to Twelves as a medium for their next challenge. He carried on from there. The British were in sympathy with his belief that something quite radical had to be done if ever there was to be another Cup match—the J boats had gone to join the Dodo. He went into court and had the deed of gift amended to lower the required minimum waterline length of 65 feet to a figure which would let the Twelves in—44 feet—and to delete the clause requiring challengers to sail on their own bottoms to the port where the race was to be held. This done, he set about organizing the syndicate which built *Columbia* and finally persuaded a reluctant Cunningham to join.

Don Matthews, not long out of Notre Dame, began the 1958 campaign as nominal skipper of the boat he had sailed often and successfully on the New York Yacht Club cruise and other occasions. However, when it became obvious that the man to make *Vim* go her fastest was Bus Mosbacher, Captain Jack did not hesitate—he had them exchange billets. The swap was accomplished without disturbing routine, without stirring resentment; it had been so natural a step to take. The more mature, experienced, and gifted Mosbacher took over direction of *Vim*'s activities. Young Don became relief helmsman and

Bus's most enthusiastic supporter. Few crews could have taken such a switch in stride.

Mosbacher was then thirty-six and on the crest of a victory wave that had swept him to eight consecutive season championships in the then white-hot International One-Design Class on Long Island Sound. He brought to his post a well-developed sense of responsibility, a realization of his new authority. He had poise, a lively sense of humor, quiet confidence in himself, and appreciatively voiced confidence in his associates. There was no part of the bucko in Mosbacher's make-up. He wore the mantle of authority easily and graciously, an indication that he possessed perhaps the most substantial quality in a Cup boat skipper: that combination of force, humanity, and magnetism called leadership.

Criticism was constructive, softly spoken, and privately given. The more upset he was about a foul up, the broader the smile, but the thinner the set of his lips. He was the epitome of politeness in these situations, but there never was any doubt in anyone's mind that he was unhappy and would not tolerate repetition of the mistake.

His crew, fully aware of what was at stake and just as fully appreciative of Mosbacher's way with a boat and the men who made it go, gave him maximum effort; they never hesitated to pass up to him any ideas they had for doing things faster, more safely, or in a manner which might save seconds in a race. Mosbacher had good men in *Vim*, very good men indeed. Some of them had sailed their own boats and thus were more accustomed to making decisions and giving orders than receiving and executing them.

From the way they worked, you never would have suspected them of having been captains. They were competent, enthusiastically cooperative hands, and seemed to enjoy the unaccustomed and temporary servitude. Good men like to sail with a good skipper; they know that if they do their jobs they can depend on him to get out of the boat all there is in her. Nothing is more discouraging to a skillful, diligent crew than to labor under the knowledge that the man at the wheel is letting them down, that they are losing races because of his technical and tactical shortcomings.

Mutual confidence and respect in skipper and crew is a prime essential to racing success—winning does not come without it in a day when men sail for the joy of the sport and a chance for glory instead of food, uniforms, laundry, and a pay envelope.

At least one boat in the 1962 trials was sorely lacking in this regard. Her crew, wearied of seeing splendid work on deck nullified by the skipper's errors, became disheartened and querulous. They continued to do their work well, nevertheless, for these were men of great pride in their competence, and they wanted to win. The nadir was reached one day when the man at the wheel in a race gave an order for a maneuver which struck his disillusioned crew as exactly the wrong thing to do in the situation. Instead of obeying instantly and without question, the key men in the evolution turned toward the cockpit and exclaimed incredulously: "*What?*"

No one who ever sailed with or against Vanderbilt, Cunningham, or Mosbacher could conceive of such a contretemps on yachts under their command. It just could not happen.

Difficulties in direction were the rule rather than the exception among the four candidates for the honor of meeting Australia's challenger. *Weatherly* alone was unaffected. In the other boats it was either too much command, or not enough; divided responsibility, or management by committee. The end result was, as always in such circumstances, failure through lack of cohesiveness and the leadership which only one man at a time can provide in any racing yacht.

Nefertiti, the only new boat built for the 1962 campaign, appeared at Newport with co-skippers: Ted Hood, the yacht's designer and sailmaker, and John McNamara, who had conceived and enterprisingly carried to fruition the idea of another Marblehead contender to share New England's Cup dreams with *Easterner*.

They were men of widely divergent temperaments and concepts of command. Hood is conservative, shy, except when relaxing with close friends, and as economical of

31

32

The smiles of victory. Bus Mosbacher, with duffle, gets a congratulatory handshake from Henry D. Mercer, head of Weatherly's owning syndicate, after sailing the defender to her concluding victory over Gretel in the 1962 series.

Olin J. Stephens II and Cornelius Shields played principal roles in Columbia's drive to the America's Cup in 1958. Stephens, who designed Columbia as a development of Vim, then also served in Columbia's afterguard. Shields was her starting helmsman in some of the trials, but his primary task was that of observer and advisor. Four years later they were with Columbia again, Stephens as navigator, Shields as observer, coach, and director of operations.

words as another famous Yankee, Calvin Coolidge. Mc-Namara, a bachelor with a taste for fast foreign sports cars, is gregarious, aggressive, volatile, and articulate.

The principals in the *Nefertiti* syndicate apparently reckoned that these antipodal young men would complement each other to the enhancement of *Nefertiti*'s chances of selection. It did not work out that way. *Nefertiti*'s performances were erratic, her crew unhappy. Before the final trials in which *Nefertiti* outlasted *Easterner* and *Columbia*, McNamara had been signed off the ship's articles and sole command assigned to Hood.

A similarly radical personnel shift was made in *Easterner* midway through the New York Yacht Club cruise. George O'Day, an amiable, ebullient Bostonian who is a champion small-boat helmsman and an Olympic gold medalist in the 5.5-Meter Class, joined the Hovey family's yacht in 1962 as helmsman and man in charge afloat. In the crew was C. Raymond Hunt, a racing skipper of long-established and lofty reputation, an inventive, nonconformist designer from whose plans *Easterner* was built, who had sailed in her in 1958 and had worked out a new keel shape for her before the 1962 season. O'Day was entirely new to Twelves in particular and big yachts in general. He set about in earnest and in his own fashion to learn his job. Like any skipper who has reached the top brackets, he had developed certain ways of doing things. Ray Hunt, another individualist, had his own ideas and his own

methods of sailing a boat. They were not even close to O'Day's.

Here again was a case of things not jelling because of a personality problem. *Easterner* was just not going. The one who went was O'Day. The Hoveys, faced with the necessity of doing something to brighten *Easterner*'s picture elected to stick with Hunt's greater experience and familiarity with the yacht.

There was no clash of personalities in *Columbia*'s afterguard, no question as to who was skipper. He was Cornelius (Glit) Shields, Jr., nephew of the man who had bought *Columbia* the summer before from the Sears syndicate, and son of Corny, Sr., one of the country's finest racing men until a heart attack suffered in a winter dinghy race restricted subsequent activities.

The elder Shields, anxious for his son to have the honor and glory which illness had made impossible for him, advised, corrected, and instructed his son, trying by some alchemy to transfer to Glit the gifts, the racing acumen, the instinct for tactics which had made him famous. Corny failed, not because he did not work hard enough

⚓

Unusual stern-to-bow view of Gretel, *the Australian challenger in 1962, rail down in dusty going, her crew lying along the weather deck. Note how hard the genoa jib is trimmed across the turnbuckles of the lee shrouds.*

34

or lacked patience and understanding, but because at twenty-seven Glit was not yet ready for the big leagues, and did not have his father's spark with people. His crew liked him as a person, but they could not give to him as skipper the unquestioning devotion that was needed.

Contrast this with how Mosbacher's shipmates felt about him. In the observation trials of 1962, *Weatherly* hit a low spot after having ticked off a string of successes. She seemed suddenly to have come unstuck. There were fumblings in execution, foul ups on deck which three times let adversaries overtake and pass her. I discussed the situation with Vic Romagna, one of *Weatherly*'s elder statesmen. A happy-go-lucky, salt-encrusted foredeck expert, who had sailed first in *Weatherly* and then in *Columbia* in 1958, and is as at home in the cabin of an ocean-racing yacht as he is in his Long Island commuter train, Romagna said: "Don't worry about *Weatherly*. We'll get going again. We've got Bus. If we don't win this thing you can bet it won't be his fault."

Mosbacher has that ingredient of character which makes him adept at handling men, enables him to build the kind of morale in a crew that welds men of widely diverse personalities, capabilities, and backgrounds into a tight, dedicated unit with an intense will to win and complete faith in their skipper's ability to do so. It is the magic catalyst which, when combined with the captain's oneness with the helm, brings an inanimate structure of wood and metal and cloth alive, transforms it into a responsive creature of grace and beauty and power.

It was thus in 1958 that *Vim* came alive, that salty, hard-bitten individualists gave so completely of themselves as a team that their nineteen-year-old, supposedly outbuilt yacht extended spanking new *Columbia* to her utmost before bowing to the boat that later ran away from Britain's *Sceptre*. Certainly no more tactically perfect, no more heart-stressing racing than that engaged in by these products of Olin J. Stephens' designing board has ever excited America's Cup trial onlookers. *Vim*'s gallant fight helped immensely to make a great defender of *Columbia*.

Rarely between sailing rivals has there been deeper respect for each other's courage and skill as that which existed between the men of *Vim* and *Columbia*. Rarely has there been a more genuine display of sportsmanship than that afforded by the spectacle of *Vim*'s crew gathered on the beach at *Columbia*'s landing, greeting their rivals with cheers when Cunningham and Sears led their men ashore after the America's Cup committee had delivered the words for which so many yearn, but so few ever hear: "Gentlemen, you have been selected . . ."

It is a swelling, soaring, unforgettable moment in the lives of everyone connected with an America's Cup candidate. More often than not even victory over the challenger is anticlimactic, for crew and captain feel that they already have caught yachting's brass ring.

For the yacht herself nothing is ever the same again. Commodore Vanderbilt expressed it so ably when he wrote after his experience with *Enterprise:* "Public interest in the America's Cup is such that when a yacht is chosen to defend it she loses her private character and becomes for the time being the property of the American people; she is their representative, their defender."

Today, from the instant his yacht is named defender, the skipper joins her in the public domain—he has no life of his own. His identity submerges in a new one forced upon him by his victory in the trials. He exists—it is hardly living—in a nightmare world of multiplying and conflicting pressures, tormented by the glare of publicity, torn between what *he* deems his responsibility and duty, and what the public regards as its due.

The pressures are cruel. Foremost is the responsibility for justifying the faith of the selection committee, of carrying out a successful defense; no one wants to go down in history as the first man to lose the Cup. Vanderbilt, Cunningham, and Mosbacher had no enthusiasm for the premise that it would be a fine thing for the sport if a challenger won for a change.

The moment the choice of defender is made the skipper's responsibility to owner, shipmates, and the yacht itself becomes a weightier burden than it was before. Having lived up to their hopes thus far, he cannot let them down when the ultimate goal is so near. Besides, there are now those millions of his countrymen who suddenly have adopted him as the standard bearer of American sailing supremacy.

He must continue, therefore, the meticulous attention to detail which made his boat the winner; study sails closely, and order recutting or the building of new ones; make certain there is no letdown in crew efficiency, or his own. He must learn what he can of his adversary's capabilities, re-check every item of rigging and gear which has the remotest possibility of failing in the big match, arrange for a haul-out for final bottom scrubbing and polishing, make certain that he has not overlooked one item, however small, which might make the defender go the slightest bit faster. A second a mile adds up to twenty-four seconds on an America's Cup course.

All this and more he must do amid the clamorous pleadings of photographers, of magazine, newsreel, radio and television interviewers, of newspaper feature writers, all seeking exclusive stories and pictures; of social climbers wanting him to be the lion in their cocktail and dinner cages; of free-loading "friends" who intrude on his one island of peace, the dinner hour relaxation with wife, shipmates, and their wives. All of these time-consuming irritations and harassments are his daily lot until the match begins. Then things become worse.

His one overriding concern should be the task of turning back the challenger and all that entails. Too often he

37

finds it difficult, if not impossible, to concentrate on this mission—at this point his one reason for being. The great American public, which discovered him only a few days earlier, will not let him.

If the skipper is gregarious, outgoing, articulate, and has an ear attuned to the trumpets of personal publicity, it is conceivable that he could or would enjoy the hurly-burly and not resent the demands on his precious time. If he is shy, uncomfortable with strangers, and/or single-minded about his racing responsibilities—and those who are not have yet to make the Cup grade—he can be nothing but miserable.

This is especially true when he is waylaid by interviewers as he comes ashore dog-tired physically, exhausted mentally (a vigorously healthy Mosbacher lost seven pounds some racing days). It might have been a particularly trying race, or a practice session in which everything went wrong. At this moment what the skipper wants most is a warm shower, leisurely cocktail, and a quiet dinner in the privacy of his quarters. Then early to bed to be fit for whatever the next day may bring.

Instead, he must summon a smile for the flashlight poppers, and patiently, lucidly answer a stream of questions, many of them irrelevancies. He begins to understand what Red Smith, *New York Herald Tribune* sports columnist, meant when he described yachting reporters as baseball writers in sneakers.

Even his living quarters afford no sanctuary. Pests, angle hustlers, and souvenir-hunting sightseers who have taken leave of their manners and common sense, if any, ignore the "Private" sign at the property gate, drive up to the house, and walk in. They want to see how a Cup crew lives, or they hope to ambush the unsuspecting skipper just when he thinks he has reached a safe haven. Some leave precipitately, urged by impatient crew members. Others walk out before they are discovered, having first taken the precaution to slip into their pockets or handbags whatever they could pick up. The situation became so appalling at Seafair, the Ocean Drive estate where *Weatherly*'s crew was quartered in 1962, that a police guard had to be established.

When the match ends, and the captain and his men have lived up to the expectations of the yacht's sponsors and the Cup committee, and have realized as well the hopes of all who had hoped for another American victory, the show is not over for the skipper; not by any means. The demands proliferate.

There are honors to receive, some real, many contrived; platitudinous speeches by the score to sit through as he

⚓

Making sail on Endeavour *was an all hands evolution. This unusual picture shows twenty men tailing on the halyard to hoist the main.*

38

listens without, he hopes, betraying his boredom. One function he will be happy to attend is the traditional America's Cup dinner of the New York Yacht Club where he will be with friends, sailing people come to pay tribute to all who had a part in the victory. His Alma Mater may do him homage, his college classmates throw a party in his honor, his old prep school ask him to address the student body. There may be a Christmas season reunion of crew, owners and wives. These are the pleasant, satisfying things the skipper will enjoy, be delighted to do because he can participate in them without wearing the hero's halo.

Unfortunately, there are other, less attractive, claims on his time, and of such a nature as to test severely his restraint. There are awards which he is expected to accept, some of them presented by organizations with only the most tenuous connection with sailboat racing, if any. There are propositions to endorse sunburn lotion, sneakers, automobiles, cigars, and liquor. There are invitations without number to appear on television shows, to lend his name to books written by ghostly hacks, to make lecture tours— to do any number of things through which someone will profit by his popularity at the expense of the skipper's self-respect and standing as an amateur yachtsman.

No one who has not been through this wringer possibly can appreciate what it means to win The Cup. The price of fame is high indeed. Only an exceptionally well-adjusted person can pay it without losing his sense of proportion or temper, lessening his love for his fellow man, and with-

out, quite excusably, becoming a cynic. Having at his side in this prolonged period of trial a tolerant, understanding wife is a godsend.

The pressures, the demands on an America's Cup captain have never been as burdensome as they are today. In the years of Vanderbilt's ascendancy there was no television. He was spared that. He could play a set or two of tennis to keep in shape without prying cameras and insistent autograph seekers cluttering the premises. At day's end he could return to his motor yacht *Vara*, anchored off the Ida Lewis Yacht Club, and play bridge with his afterguard without fear of being disturbed. Uninvited visitors were not welcome at the gangway. There were no telephones or doorbells to answer—nor any necessity for hiding the table silver, ash trays, and bric-a-brac from acquisitive sightseers.

Even in 1958 things were by no means as bad as they were four years later. Twenty-one years and a world war had passed since the *Ranger-Endeavour II* match closed the J boat chapter of America's Cup history, and the resumption of Britain versus U.S.A. rivalry off Newport caught the news media off guard. Many newspaper, magazine, and picture editors either had never heard of the America's Cup, or forgotten about it. Few persons then

⚓

T. O. M. Sopwith at the wheel of Endeavour with Mrs. Sopwith looking aloft—perhaps for divine inspiration.

40

active in the writing profession had ever seen a Cup race, much less reported one. Consequently, the curtain was about to go up on yachting's big show before many of the communications executives awoke to its significance. Then they discovered that making contact with the principals was not easy.

Columbia's crew was quartered in a big house on a walled estate overlooking Brenton Cove, where the competing yachts and much of the spectator fleet were moored. The high wall and heavy iron gates were discouraging, and, because the establishment had its own pier on the cove, all hands could go to and from *Columbia* and her tender without running the gantlet of the public and its agents. *Sceptre*'s headquarters were even less accessible, tucked away as they were in a remote corner of Conanicut Island, half an hour's ferry ride from Newport.

In 1962 the heat was on constantly. There were so many domestic and foreign correspondents and cameramen in Newport that the city government and the New York Yacht Club established a headquarters for them in an old armory on Thames Street. There were held post-race press conferences. *Gretel*'s skipper, Jock Sturrock, was spared the task of appearing at them because the head of his syndicate, Sir Frank Packer, Australian press, television, and radio magnate, was opposed to participation in such gatherings. He relented to the extent of designating one of *Gretel*'s stand-by crew, Doug Fairfax, as the challenger's

spokesman. It was no surprise that the amiable, but restrained Mr. Fairfax imparted little startling information.

Mosbacher deputized George O'Day, who had joined the *Weatherly* camp after parting from *Easterner*, to represent him at the conference. After one appearance, George unthinkingly disqualified himself as U.S. spokesman by writing something in a Boston newspaper—he doubled as a temporary author—which aroused the ire of the Packer camp. Whereupon, *Weatherly*'s skipper himself took over the day that *Gretel* won her only race and tied the series. After that, Bus's younger brother, Bobby, talked for the family until the big finale when Bus joined Sturrock on the podium.

When it was all over in 1958, it was literally just that. Cunningham, not a free-and-easy mixer, but a person who detests show of any kind and intensely dislikes public speaking, is not the type whom program directors, publicists, and peddlers approach more than once. For that reason, and the fact that outside pressures were not as thoroughly organized then as they were in 1962, Cunningham got off lightly.

It was so different when *Weatherly* was the defender that there must have been many times when Mosbacher asked himself bitterly whether being a Cup defense skipper was worth the candle. At lunch with friends two days after the match had been concluded he said: "I've had it. Never again." And he meant it.

THE CREW

Supporting Cast for the Star

As the support of a competent cast is essential to a fine performance by a theatrical headliner, and clever receivers are indispensable to the best of football forward passers, so the man at the wheel of a racing yacht must be the pivot of a precisely coordinated ensemble skilled in the art and mechanics of sail setting, trimming, and shifting.

Much has been written about team effort as a requisite of victory in sports competition. Rarely is this more true than in the task of making an America's Cup boat sail up to her potential and, under extreme competitive pressure, beyond it.

A clever actor can cover a missed cue; a quick, nimble runner can make football yardage despite inept blocking; but the racing helmsman has not been born who can execute a successful back-winding tack under an adversary's lee bow, if the man whose job it is to lead the jibsheet around the winch drum lets the line slip out of his grasp.

In a close race, one missed assignment, one foul up under stress, tips the balances. The fastest yacht, the most gifted skipper cannot win with a lubberly deck gang.

Crews are never 100 per cent efficient in every maneuver in every race; they are subject to the same human tendency to err as athletes in any other game of precision. But the sailing organization that comes closest to perfection usually is the one whose captain collects the trophies. America's Cup history shouts from the main truck that the United States always has had finely drilled, dependably effective, and highly competitive crews to go with first-rate skippers and fast yachts.

Until the Cup deed of gift was revised to bring the relatively small 12-Meter Class yachts into the picture in 1958, crews for defenders and defense candidates were recruited from professional seamen—hands from Scandinavian windships, State-of-Mainers from fishing and coasting schooner fleets. In this generation, virtually all are amateurs, many fresh from the one-design, small-boat racing classes, some hardened in the rougher life of taking ocean racers down to the sea.

Their normal occupations may or may not be nautical. In a typical boat you might find the operator of a highly sophisticated electronic computer cranking a winch with a husky college athlete, an insurance salesman being hoisted aloft in a bosun's chair by a lawyer, a liquor drummer helping a banker to sweat in the mainsheet, a stevedoring company executive taking compass bearings, an artist teaming with a shopkeeper in setting the spinnaker.

Sailmakers, yacht designers, shipyard proprietors, and others whose financial welfare is linked to the sport often are included in Cup boat crews, but only if they have something more to contribute than their specialties. They are signed on for the same reason as everyone else—because they are thoroughly dedicated, competent yachtsmen first and professional or businessmen some other time when it does not interfere with sailing. The question of professionalism is not present because in American yachting a man is not considered to be a professional sailor unless he draws wages for sailing.

Twelve-Meter crews reflect accurately the yachting mores of our times. A man's method of gaining a livelihood does not matter on a boat, nor does his social standing or Dun and Bradstreet rating. The standard of acceptance is this: What kind of a shipmate is he, how well does he perform his seaman's tasks?

These men of diverse economic, educational, and occupational backgrounds are brought together by one common denominator—love of the sea and sailing ships. All of their other qualifications for billets in America's Cup yacht crews are erected on that base, for if they did not find in sailboats and sailboat-racing people something they could find nowhere else, they would not make the sacrifices they do to sail the Twelves.

Leo H. (Buddy) Bombard, a little man of great courage and a tremendous capacity for enjoying yachting in all of its forms, senses something almost mystical in the experience of racing a good boat with a good crew. He likens it in many respects to skiing and flying, and he has done both, one in the New Hampshire hills in his student days at Dartmouth, the other when he was an Air Force jet pilot.

"You need," he says, "the same precision, the same sense of timing. In all three the reaction is the same: If you don't do something quite right it doesn't feel good. If you do, well it's simply wonderful, really exalting." He spent at least two summers of his active young life feeling simply wonderful and at times exalted. He served in *Vim* in 1958 and *Weatherly* in 1962.

Cup boat crews which experience the mystique of perfection afloat don't just happen; they are put together and tuned as carefully as the yachts in which they sail. The most efficient deck organizations are those with the correct balance of experience and youth, specialization and versatility, skill and muscle, enthusiasm and depth of purpose. Just as no football team can hope for success if it has eleven halfbacks on the field at once, or a business prosper if it has five accountants and only one salesman, so a Cup boat crew must have the right men in the proper quantities for specific jobs, not merely the requisite number of bodies.

Where does a skipper or yacht owner look for muscle men to pump winches and heave on halyards; quick, nimble, knowledgeable sailors to supervise foredeck and amidships operations; men with a knack for sail trimming;

⚓

Captain George Monsell, his mates, and Ranger's *professional crew (22 all told) pose formally for their team picture on the foredeck.*

46

navigators; and the adaptable, all-round experienced hands who can do any job on deck and do it well?

They are easy to find. Our coastal harbors and the Great Lakes yachting centers abound in young men and more mature but by no means old sailors, who have solid small-boat racing backgrounds and enough alongshore or offshore experience in larger craft to be seamen in the best sense of the word and therefore familiar with big-boat gear, its care, and handling.

Assuming proper qualification in these respects and the physical condition needed to stand up to a season of almost constant, day-long drilling and racing, what other attributes must a candidate for a Cup boat crew possess?

For the answer, we return to the team factor, cohesiveness in spirit and effort, and the element which is its catalyst. Bus Mosbacher, who certainly knows, and Palmer Sparkman, whose qualifications include service under three 12-Meter skippers in three dissimilar crews, place compatibility number one on the list.

Nothing, they say, is more important in a sailor's make-up than the ability to work, play, and live harmoniously with persons of other age groups, backgrounds, responsibilities, and tastes; nothing is more essential than the adaptability and thoughtfulness which earn for the possessor the mariner's accolade: "He is a fine shipmate."

Bachelors and men with growing families, college graduates and men who have succeeded in their vocations with limited formal education, old yachting hands and comparative youngsters, extroverts, practical jokers, studious types, comics, and straight men, smokers and nonsmokers, beer drinkers, chaps who prefer cocktails, some whose refreshment never is stronger than ginger ale—you will find all of them in any Cup boat crew.

They get along well together because the less experienced members listen to and learn from their elders, and the latter impart knowledge and guidance without talking down to their younger shipmates. Mutual respect, tolerance for the tastes and mannerisms of others, compatibility go hand in hand.

One abrasive character, one habitual shirker of unpleasant or routine tasks, one of too thin a skin to accept in good part the bantering which is an inevitable part of life among healthy, active people, can throw an entire organization out of tune. No matter how well qualified he may be technically, if his mates find it difficult to adjust to him, the skipper will be well advised to sign him off the ship's articles.

The next important crew requirement on Mosbacher's

⚓

Part of Ranger's *winning team: Commodore Vanderbilt with his afterguard, left to right—Rod Stephens, Olin Stephens, Professor Zenas Bliss (the navigator), Mrs. Vanderbilt, the Commodore, and Arthur Knapp, Jr.*

list is time; time, that is, to devote four months or so to a single-minded quest for selection as defender of the America's Cup. In this connection, a sympathetic boss is indispensable. In some cases "boss" should be written "wife." Wives of men who join Cup boat crews are a special breed. They are especially tolerant, understanding young women, who are willing to stay home with the children, take over the responsibility of running the household on a reduced budget, and give up a husband's companionship so that he can sail in what may well turn out to be a hopeless cause, but one which he nevertheless feels he must support with all the skill, experience, and courage he possesses.

For college students, sailing in a defense candidate is largely a matter of taking a different type of vacation, but it means giving up all other racing activities, social contacts, family associations, and in some cases delaying the search for a job.

For those who have established themselves in careers, the problems are not always easily solved. The employer must be cooperative and give the necessary leave of absence —it helps if he happens to be a yachting buff. If there is a family to consider, the question of getting along without a regular pay check arises. The miracle is that whenever the call goes out so many are able to make the necessary adjustments and keep all concerned reasonably happy for the duration of the campaign.

The layman often asks: "Who selects the crew? How does he go about it?" There is no pat answer. Like most elements of Cup boat operation, the method of recruiting differs from boat to boat. The waterfront crimp went out of style in this country when the seamen's union hiring halls came in, and certainly there is no employment agency equipped to furnish in one neat, promptly delivered package the personnel for a 12-Meter crew.

Sometimes syndicates pick their men in committee, more frequently they appoint a manager and leave this task and many others to him. Generally, the owner rounds up the crew in consultation with his skipper. The best way is to give the skipper full responsibility in the matter.

He has to sail with those chosen, *he* has to weld them into an efficient unit, and *he* must have full confidence in them as individuals and as a working organization. His is the reputation at stake when the competition begins; any failures, any weaknesses will be laid at his door—not at that of the owner, who insisted that his dilettante nephew be taken aboard, or of the syndicate chairman, who rewarded a generous contributor by foisting him off on the skipper

⚓

Contrast the two photographs of Ranger's *crew with this one of* Weatherly's *entire complement—skipper, afterguard, deckhands, "bench," and port engineer. The photograph opposite undoubtedly was taken after a winning race.*

50

as an expert at trimming headsails. Helmsmen also have mortal limitations.

Let us assume that the yachtsman who has taken command of a Cup defense candidate also has carte blanche in the selection of his shipmates. He begins, naturally enough, among his sailing friends whose equipment for the task ahead he knows well. Usually they are yachtsmen with whom he has raced, probably offshore, or seamen from other ships whom he encountered on the deep-water racing circuit, liked the cut of their jibs, liked what he heard about them.

He leans toward ocean-racing men for a very good reason. The America's Cup match and most of the trials leading up to it are sailed on the open sea. He must have good seamen accustomed to doing their work in all kinds of weather and at all hours, on a wet, unstable, heaving platform, and never permitting physical fatigue to interfere with getting things done.

With blue-water sailing men courage and strong stomachs are assumed. They also will have that most important quality, compatibility. If they had been lacking in this characteristic, it is certain that they would not have sailed in a good ocean racer more than once.

Telephone calls to one or two prospects, luncheons with others and a letter to one not readily accessible, start the skipper on his way to lining up the key men in his organization, those who will share some of his responsibilities and on whom he will rely for advice. In the latter respect he may begin early, asking members of his nucleus for their opinions of sailors he might be considering for deck assignments, or for outright recommendations of personnel.

Bob Welch was one member of *Weatherly*'s 1962 crew who owed his berth to just such a testimonial. Welch was virtually unknown in the Long Island sailing fraternity. He had won no small-boat racing championships, nor had he stood watches in winning ocean racers, but he had been with Buddy Bombard in *Columbia* for a while in 1961. Bombard was one of the first of Mosbacher's choices for his 1962 crew. And Bombard, praising his candidate's character, attitude, strength, loyalty, and adaptability, persuaded his skipper to give Welch a trial. Mosbacher did and Welch made the grade.

Once the first-line operatives, the specialists, are in the fold it is relatively easy to fill in the chinks around them with material carefully screened from the bulging ranks of those who regard the opportunity to sail in a Cup

⚓

Defender (1895). Sailors in those days earned their wages wrestling with heavy, bulky canvas. Here two mates on the foredeck are supervising half a dozen hands engaged in the task of clearing sheets and getting a jib hanked onto its stay.

defense candidate as nothing short of heaven. Only those who have done it know how often it is quite the opposite, but they are always eager to do it again.

The ideal 12-Meter boat deckhand is in his twenties, sturdily framed, well muscled, personable, adaptable, and brimming with enthusiasm for a sport in which he has participated half his life, part of it, perhaps, as skipper of his own little boat. He has a lively sense of humor as well as responsibility, he is self-reliant and self-disciplined. Perfect candidates, fitting this description, are by no means as rare as you might think. Decks of the flotilla at Newport were studded with them in the summer of the Australian challenge.

Putting a 12-Meter crew together for a Cup venture is not unlike laying out squares on a sheet of paper, labeling each with the appropriate job title, and then writing in a name whose owner fits the job. Let's start forward of the mast and draw blocks on the deck outline as we work aft to the cockpit, filling in the billets' requirements as we go.

There must be a foredeck expert, a seasoned sailorman skilled in the art of getting the most lift and pull out of the huge nylon balloons known in the sailing trade as spinnakers, competent, sure-handed, and quick in the changing and trimming of headsails, tireless in his concentration.

Teamed with him should be a strong, big-muscled youth

to man the jib and spinnaker halyards, help manhandle the spinnaker pole, and get sails up on deck, and a knowing, meticulous, level-headed seaman who checks everything—makes certain that shackles are closed, sheets led properly, halyards coiled for running, blocks in the right locations, and everything clear for the operation about to be performed.

Amidships is the 12-Meter's "engine room." Here are located the big pedestal winches which sailors call "coffee grinders." These are the crank-activated capstans used for sheeting home genoa jibs and heaving around on the guys controlling the fore and aft position of the spinnaker pole. The emphasis in this department is on power— power in the equipment and power in its human operators. Winch grinders must be superbly conditioned young men of exceptional strength and stamina. They are the crew members on whom the greatest physical demands are made when rival yachts engage in protracted short-tacking duels, especially in strong breezes. It is quite common in such nautical dogfights to come about as many as fifteen

⚓

In the morning, before there is any sailing, there's work to be done in the pierside shed. Weatherly's crew is picking up the thick, heavy sausage-roll of the mainsail which will have to be carried down the pier to their vessel and then bent onto the boom.

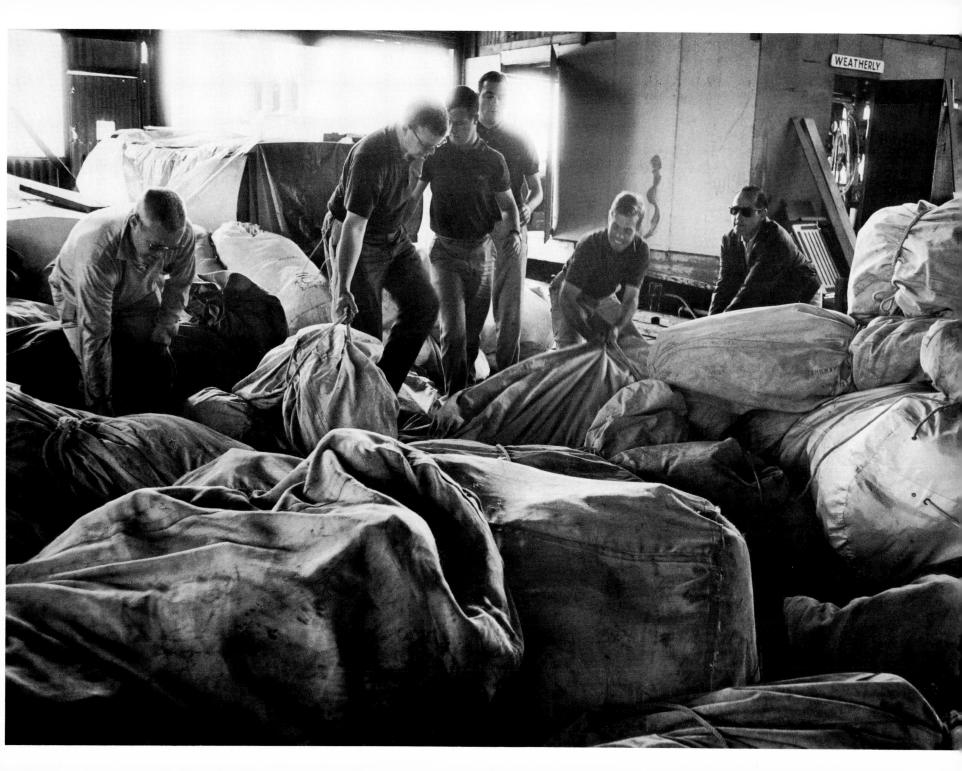

times with scarcely a deep breath between. Such short tacking duels were uncommon with the larger J boats.

It takes deep reserves of strength to carry winch crankers through such ordeals. Men have coughed up blood, and there were occasions in the early 1962 trials, before peak condition was attained, when some 'midships hands were so exhausted after fiercely contested races in which a multitude of tacks were made that they remained abed the next morning and standbys took their places on board.

With the winchmen are paired "tailers," men with quick hands and a sharp sense of timing whose job it is to get the proper number of turns of the jibsheet on the winch drum when the boat is being put over from one tack to the other and then take in the slack smartly by hauling hand over hand on the dacron rope tail of the wire which controls the set of the headsail.

The "tailers" do this as the winchmen grind the sheet in, first rapidly by the yard with arms flailing like pistons, then slower and slower, painful inch by painful inch, gasping for breath as muscles strain against thousands of pounds of wind pressure in the big sail. Those last hard-won clicks on the winch are vital to getting the jib flattened to its most effective aerodynamic shape.

Aft, one on deck or both in the cockpit depending on how the equipment is installed, two more men are needed to handle the mainsheet, and the backstay runners which support the 90-foot tall aluminum mast at the point where the jibstay exerts its tremendous forward pull. One of these men, normally the one whose primary assignment is tending backstays, serves as the skipper's eyes, ears, and voice when the helmsman is concentrating on making the boat move. He listens for word being passed aft by the crew, relays orders forward, all the while keeping his eyes on the enemy so as not to be caught napping by a quick maneuver, and watching for signs of a wind shift. This sailor should also be sufficiently skilled in steering to relieve the helm whenever the skipper needs a break.

The real specialist in the crew is the navigator; the others all ought to be able to do at least one other job besides that to which they are assigned on the station bill. The navigator's sole but towering responsibility is to tell the captain exactly where the boat is at any time, what the heading is to the next mark, which way the tidal current is setting, how long to hold a tack before coming about to fetch a turning buoy, and, with the stadimeter's help, how much they are gaining or losing with relation to the adversary's position.

The importance of a high degree of competence in a

⚓

Nefertiti had her problems early in the 1962 trials. Skipper Ted Hood keeps the husky Marblehead boat moving as amidships' winch grinders and sheet tailers work to clear a jam on the winch drum.

One of the day's first tasks for the crew of a Cup candidate is bending on the mainsail. Here Buddy Bombard guides the sail onto the boom track while two of his Weatherly shipmates haul it aft.

Teamwork on Columbia's jibsheet. As the tailer (left) takes in the slack, winchmen on the "coffee grinder" make the winch handles whirr.

There's one on every 12-Meter, a light but strong, extremely nimble young man whose job it is to go aloft any time and clear things when lines become fouled. These photographs show Easterner's aerialist aloft, while a race is in progress, to clear a spinnaker guy led to the wrong side of the jibstay. The acrobatics involved shinnying up the spinnaker pole by way of its downhaul, and fishing with the legs for the foreguy as a preliminary to descent.

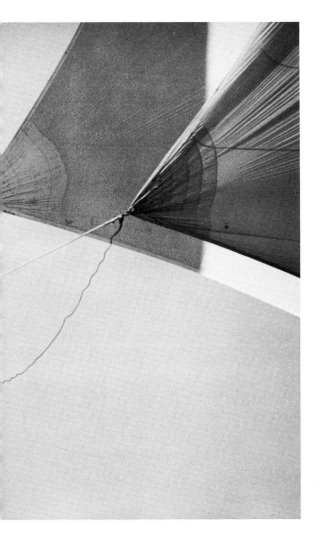

The race is over and won, but the day's work for Weatherly's *crew* isn't done—*not until the battens are pulled out of their pockets and the mainsail is slid off the boom and stowed below. The flag flying in the starboard rigging is an affirmative reply to the race committee's signaled query: "Do you consent to racing the next weekday?"*

Keeping an America's Cup candidate in peak racing condition is a never-ending task. A working party from Columbia *trucks one of her coffee grinder winches to the shop for overhaul. No one on board is exempt from this kind of labor, not even afterguard members, in this case Johnny Nichols (second from left) and Olin Stephens, Columbia's designer and navigator (second from right).*

navigator is borne out by the fact that many a race has been lost by overstanding the weather buoy, or by fetching a few lengths short of it and having to make an extra short tack to get around, and by sailing too high or too low of the proper course on a reaching leg. You don't have to go back in Cup history any farther than the 1962 trials for examples of all of these mistakes. And *Gretel* dimmed her chances against *Weatherly* in the first race of the 1962 match by widely overstanding the weather mark on the first round.

A baseball team which cannot call on skilled relief pitchers, lacks utility infielders and outfielders, reliable pinch hitters and runners, and all of the rest of the reserve personnel which managers call their "bench" cannot win in the major leagues. Neither can a football team without depth in its replacements. A Cup yacht's success depends to a lesser degree on its "bench," but it must have such a bulwark, one in which the emphasis is on high quality and low numbers. The more personnel, the more headaches for those in charge.

How many spare hands and auxiliary personnel are acquired depends on the owner's or syndicate manager's approach to the manning problem and that of continuing development of the boat as a racing machine. Accidents do occur on the best of boats, and even sailors fall ill; family or business matters sometimes require brief absences. In these emergencies a standby member of the organization must be prepared to step into the vacancy and fill it without adverse effect on team efficiency.

Sailing yachts without auxiliary power—and Twelves are in this category—need tenders to tow them out of the harbor to the race course and back. The tenders also carry extra sails, tools, and spare gear, and provide a mobile platform from which the reserve personnel can learn by observation.

Last, but far from the least important on the roster, is the most substantial nonracing member of the organization —the port captain, port engineer, shipyard coordinator, or whatever the shoreside jack-of-all-trades is titled. He should be a naval architect and engineer. If he is also a sailor, so much the better. Someone like Paul Coble, for example, who took care of *Columbia*'s yard needs in 1958 after working on her plans under Olin Stephens. Or like *Weatherly*'s invaluable Edgar Bainbridge, project engineer, consultant, machinist, carpenter, rigging specialist, purchasing agent, and no one knows what else in the 1962 campaign. Alan Payne, *Gretel*'s creator, was all of these and more to the Australian organization.

With the acquisition of such a stalwart, the complement is filled. Then begins the task of fitting all of the pieces together, smoothing rough edges, adding here, taking away there. It is the sort of endeavor that never really seems to end, at least not before the final match has been sailed.

DEVELOPING THE TEAM

How a Winning Combination Is Put Together

American skippers may differ in their methods, but their actions reveal agreement on the principle that the sooner a crew can be trained into an effective working unit, the sooner the commanders will have reduced the importance of the human element among the imponderables connected with the development of a new yacht, or one which has undergone major changes.

Because the rate of crew progress from a heterogeneous state to that of an efficiently functioning whole is so vital to the success of an America's Cup campaign, most planning is, or should be, based on getting the boat overboard and rigged as early in the spring as possible. Sailing time is of the essence no matter which approach is taken toward solution of personnel problems.

While everyone agrees on the seriousness and thoroughness with which a crew should be organized, there is a diversity of opinion as to how to go about it. There are three principal modes of procedure, and at one time or another all have produced the desired result: a closely knit, finely tuned, highly competitive ship's company dedicated to making their yacht go faster than the adversary's.

Some skippers carefully build a crew in advance and stay with it come hell or high water. A second method, really a modification of the first, is to predetermine the make-up of the ship's afterguard and deck gang, and then tack onto the roster two or three alternates who can be worked in at the skipper's option, or when the occasion demands. The third, and least desirable from the point of view of the individuals concerned, is to recruit more deckhands than needed and then weed out until the skipper settles on the few who meet his standards. The purpose behind this last procedure is to stimulate competition among an abundance of eager candidates for whatever posts are available and thus attain a high level of competence among the survivors. From the captain's eminence this may be ideal, but there is no denying that it works a hardship on those who are not selected. There is nowhere for them to go. It is too late under normal circumstances for them to join one of the other Cup yachts, and, having made arrangements for a long absence, it may be impossible, or at least difficult, to return to business right away.

Hand-picking crews well before launching day has the distinct advantage of giving the men a longer period afloat as a unit, more time in which to dovetail their skills and seamen's instincts into the pattern of team effort that is the hallmark of all good sailing organizations. A crew of this type will be much farther advanced in development in the early trials than one which is still in a state of flux, and oftentimes the later starters never overhaul the earlier formed unit.

Vim's 1958 crew is an excellent example of a preformed group which got the jump on its rivals and was caught only by the *Weatherly* side—another hand-picked outfit. Because *Vim*'s deck organization was so far ahead of *Columbia*'s in development, the older and slower boat was able to give the new vessel the scare of her life before she was named defender. And *Columbia*'s men will tell you unhesitatingly that they never reached their peak as a crew until it was almost too late.

Columbia, be it noted, always had extra hands and was moving them into and out of the boat right up to and including her match with *Sceptre*. The latter, incidentally, was one of those "fight-for-the-jobs-boys" adherents, and waited until well into the summer before settling on the make-up of her crew.

However crew organization is tackled, it is essential that decisions on personnel be made with the minimum of delay, so that the maximum time for perfecting and polishing teamwork is possible.

In 1962 two of the Cup defense organizations began the season with many more deckhands than they could use at one time, and they ended it with some spares. *Weatherly*, as in most matters of operating policy, differed from her rivals. She took a leaf from the *Vim* and *Weatherly* books of 1958. When she began sailing in May, she carried only one spare hand and he was a young man who had been signed on specifically for that role. Billy Kelly had no company on the bench until the final trials when *Weatherly*'s reserves were augmented by three men who volunteered their services as stand-bys after having been cut

from the rosters of other Cup defense candidates. As things turned out, their dismissals opened the way to good fortune.

Mosbacher neither conducted eliminations nor kept candidates dangling. He believed it unfair to ask yachtsmen to give up a whole summer of business or vacation on the off-chance that they might be picked for his team. In his view, it is the skipper's responsibility to pick the right men before the season begins and then carry through with them. If he has made any inadvisable choices then the fault is the selector's, not that of the selectee.

When Mosbacher signed on George O'Day, an *Easterner* cast-off, and Bob Derecktor and Bob Gibson, who did not fit into the *Columbia* setup, he made it plain to all hands that the acquisition of this able trio was strictly an insurance measure, that no changes were contemplated in the crew which had sailed *Weatherly* so well all summer. The pale blue boat went through the do-or-die trials against *Nefertiti* with the same men who were aboard when she did her spring practice in Long Island Sound.

Weatherly was fortunate in that she never had an emergency which required the services of her reserve deckhand, but when the strategic and administrative situ-

⚓

Wet work for part of Gretel's *crew assigned to getting their weight over the weather rail in the one rough weather race of the 1962 Cup match.*

Gretel's *men proving that manpower, even in these days*
of mechanized yachts, is still vital, especially in heavy going.
Here they sweat down the outhaul of the mainsail clew.

The canvas "skirt" around the mainmast covers cleats and winches so that jibsheets won't foul on them when the ship is being tacked or jibed.

The foredeck gang getting a jib off the stay. The man sitting on the pulpit, his back to where Gretel is going, unhanks the sail while four others smother and bundle it preparatory to sending it below.

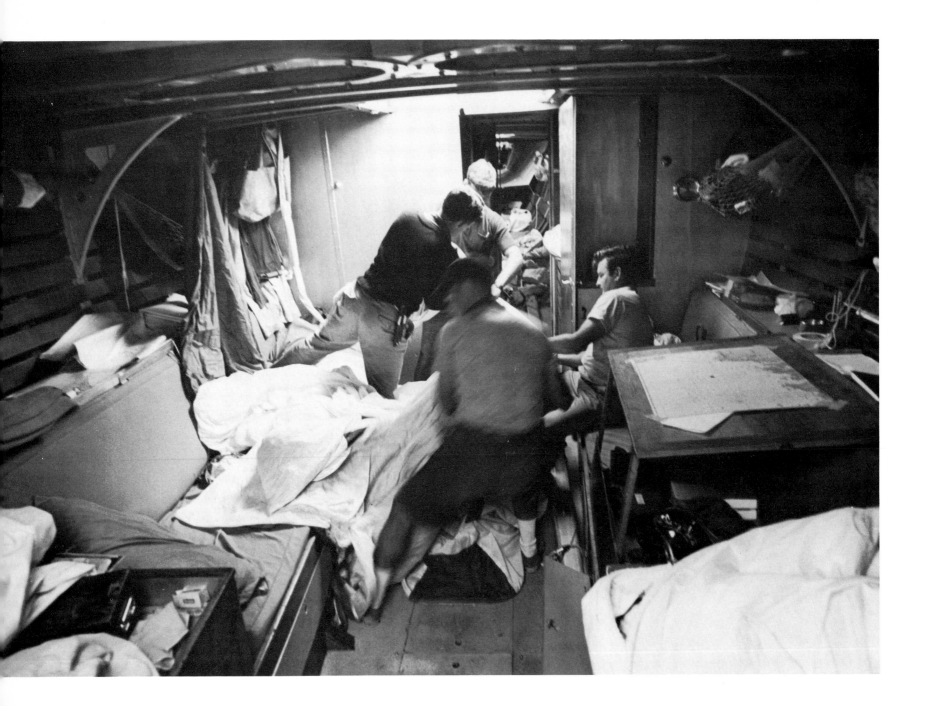

No rest below. Columbia seamen putting a jib in stops in the cabin to get it ready to send aloft again.

This view from Columbia's bow shows her hard on the wind approaching the weather mark and all squared away for the ensuing downwind leg. The spinnaker "turtle," or container, is secured to the port footrail and the spinnaker pole's inboard end is in the bell near the foot of the mast, ready to be hoisted to starboard as the kite goes up. The crew, having done all it can in anticipation of the next maneuver, relaxes on the midships line for a moment.

ations suggested a change in the cockpit after *Gretel* had beaten her in the second race, Mosbacher went to what he repeatedly praised as "the strongest bench in the league." He moved O'Day from that bench to the executive officer's billet in the cockpit, and *Weatherly* ran out the match with three victories in a row.

In Australia, the Royal Sydney Yacht Squadron syndicate backing the *Gretel* venture had had no choice of method in finding a crew to man the continent's first challenger from down under.

That country had no 12-Meter yachts, nor had it ever raced an International Rule vessel larger than an 8-Meter. Neither had any of its amateur mariners ever sailed one. Australia was starting from scratch in both departments. With characteristic enterprise, the syndicate solved its problems with one stroke: It chartered *Vim* from Captain Matthews and had her shipped to Sydney with her fine professional captain, Willie Carstens. *Vim* served a dual purpose—she gave Alan Payne a point of departure for the design of *Gretel*, and she provided a training medium for those who hoped to be chosen for the challenger's crew.

Two full crews with spares were recruited from the ranks of Australia's small-boat racers and offshore seamen. They were organized into separate teams, outfitted in different uniforms, and set to the task of learning from Willie how to operate a racing machine of *Vim*'s size and complexity. They learned quickly, but naturally had to

divide their time between boat and beach because there was only one boat to sail.

After *Gretel* was launched, development proceeded more rapidly for now both groups were afloat continuously. They alternated between *Vim* and the new boat, and rivalry between the teams grew so intense that the older hands had to cool the hotter heads. When *Vim* and *Gretel* arrived in the United States to do the challenger's final tuning in the waters she would sail with the defender, the crew units were flown over to join them.

As the time to make a choice between teams drew nearer, the Australian brain trust decided that a better crew than either could be organized from personnel drawn from both. Then began a shuffling process. Men were tried in different combinations until a week before the match with *Weatherly*. Then the crew was chosen—a fine deck organization, superbly conditioned, smart in execution of all evolutions, and completely competent in all respects. No challenger ever had a better one, and its merits matched those of our best.

Training methods probably differ as much if not more than the ways in which crews are organized. Formal physical training sessions were an integral part of the Australians' daily routine. American skippers left the job of getting into and remaining in condition up to the individual. While their counterparts from Melbourne and Sydney and Brisbane were doing mass calisthenics on the dewy lawn of their Castle Hill headquarters before breakfast every morning, Yankee sailors were taking their exercise in the form of pounding pillows with their ears.

The better method of conditioning Cup boat crews—rigidly controlled hours and surpervised gymnastics *versus* elective exertion as a supplement to that involved in the repeated tacking and jibing of a large sailing vessel—is purely a matter of choice, since both appear to achieve the same result. The eighteenth match for the America's Cup demonstrated that beyond a doubt.

The Australians were fine sailors and fierce competitors. They never defeated *Weatherly* on a windward leg, and they never stopped trying to get out from under her lee.

By precipitating sustained tacking duels—the usual tactic of a trailing boat trying to shake the enemy off her wind—the Australians sought to break the Americans down, induce the fatigue which destroys timing and leads to foul ups. They failed. The tall, muscular Australian athletes, who looked as though they could step into the offensive line of the Green Bay Packers on a moment's notice, found their equals in staying power in the less physically prepossessing men on *Weatherly*'s emery board deck.

It is important to consider in this connection the fact that the Aussies had the mechanical advantage of *Gretel*'s linked winches which enabled four men at a time to crank in her genoa jibsheet whereas only two could do it on *Weatherly*'s independent coffee grinders.

The only time *Weatherly* broke off a tacking fight was in the second race, a heavy-weather slogging match, which *Gretel* won on the last downhill leg. Finding himself down in *Weatherly*'s backwind shortly after the start, Jock Sturrock, *Gretel*'s skipper, went into the short tacking routine. True to the book, Mosbacher covered, tack for tack. It soon became obvious that *Weatherly* was losing ground. *Gretel*, with her teamed winches, was able to sheet in her headsail faster and settle onto the new tack quicker than the American boat. So Mosbacher broke off the duel, not because his winch grinders could not take the punishment of continuous tacking in a strong breeze, but because there was no sense in playing—and losing—*Gretel*'s game when, by sailing his own race, he could hold his weather position. The wisdom of Mosbacher's decision to leave *Gretel* to her own devices was borne out by the fact that *Weatherly* rounded the windward mark first in that race, as she did in every other one.

⚓

"Ready about!" comes the helmsman's order and Gretel's *crew moves quickly, smoothly to tacking stations.*

⚓

"Hard-a-lee!" comes the command of execution, and Gretel *flips over to the starboard tack after* Weatherly, *who is shown crossing her bow, had tacked onto her wind.*

77

Gretel's crew began each day at 6:30 A.M. The men rolled out of their bunks on "The Rock," their nickname for the Australian establishment on Castle Hill, and forthwith fell into formation on the grass in front of the hotel to do pushups, deep knee bends, situps, and other muscle-building exercises before topping off the calisthenics with some hill-and-dale roadwork over the paths which interlace the fields, crags, and thickets of the property.

After a shower and breakfast everyone repaired to Port O' Call, where *Gretel* and *Vim* were moored. They performed a multitude of chores and eventually went sailing, quite often not returning until almost dark. Then all hands went back to Castle Hill for dinner preceded, not by cocktails, but by the daily ration of two beers per man. After that the Australians were on their own until 11:30 curfew time and bed check.

In contrast to this regimen, the American way of doing things seemed slack. It may have been so in appearance, but in practice it was hardly that. The essential difference was in the fact that ways and means of maintaining sound physical condition was left to the individual. Hours were regular, but there were no masters-at-arms checking on the sailors, and the kind of tipple a man imbibed, or how much, was his own responsibility. If there were any abuses of this privilege, they never reached the ears of Thames Street gossips.

Instead of building muscle and lung power by cadenced exercises—as a leader grunted: "One-Two. One-Two. One-Two. Halt!"—the Americans sailed themselves into fitness. Hour upon hour, day after day, week in, week out, before, between, and after trial series, they were out in their boats, incessantly tacking and jibing, heaving and hauling. Legs, arms, shoulders, and backs were strengthened for the strains of combat by going through the same movements in practice as they would in a race. The principle involved is that which governs oarsmen whose condition and technical proficiency usually is in direct ratio to the number of hours spent in rowing machines and shells. Oarsmen row themselves into shape, sailors sail themselves into shape.

The parallel between rowing and sailing was even closer for a brief time in 1962. Don McNamara, *Nefertiti*'s co-skipper at that time, thought it would be a good idea for candidates for her crew to get themselves into condition before her launching by swinging sweeps in rowing shells on the Charles. It was tried and then abandoned, probably because so few shared Don's enthusiasm for the galley slave aspects of the drill. It wasn't fun. Don, a football player in his undergraduate days at Harvard, then installed training methods identified with that sport.

Every man in the crew was assigned a number which was sewn on his racing jersey. When *Nefertiti* took her early practice spins at Marblehead, a motion picture cameraman followed closely in a tender to photograph all evolutions. The film, developed and printed overnight, was shown at a crew critique held before the next drill, much as game movies are run off for football squads. Mistakes in technique or execution were caught by the camera's sharp eye and there was no escape for the responsible man—that was his number, wasn't it?

Meanwhile *Weatherly* just sailed and sailed and sailed.

The result was steady improvement in execution; things were done with greater speed and more precision. Bodies grew stronger and harder. By August no Australian had a flatter abdomen than Charley Bertrand, one of *Weatherly's* "engineers," nor tougher, stronger arm muscles than Ned Hall, the foredeck Atlas. Buddy Bombard looked like a small, thin-faced boy alongside his opposite number in *Gretel*, but if there was a more nimble, more gifted, more durable 'midships division officer in the fleet that summer, he does not come to mind.

If any Yankee felt he was not getting enough work afloat to make him glad to fall into bed before eleven o'clock, he was at liberty to take more exercise of his own choosing. Extemporaneous touch football games were popular on days when there was no sailing. Hiking or running back to their quarters, instead of automobile riding, was the ploy of a few *Columbians*. Palmer Sparkman, for one, and Bob Derecktor, for another, used to run the mile from their yacht's berth in the Newport Shipyard to the crew's home up the hill behind Brenton Cove, lugging sailbags stuffed with gear.

In 1958, England's training methods more closely resembled the American than the Australian. Discipline was self-imposed—grown men with a mission were presumed to know how to take care of themselves—and there was heavy emphasis on competitive sailing. *Sceptre's* men sailed forty-three tests against her trial horse, the prewar 12-Meter *Evaine,* and forty of these were crowded between the end of May and late July, when she was hauled out preparatory to being shipped to New York. After her arrival at Newport, *Sceptre* continued her match racing with the 1937-vintage American Twelve, *Gleam,* as her opponent.

When *Sceptre* came to the line for her first race with *Columbia,* her crew was ready for whatever demands might be made on it. The fact that *Sceptre* was soundly trounced four times running was in no measure attributable to deficiencies in crew performance. As a boat the challenger simply was not in *Columbia's* class, nor, for that matter, in that of any of the 1958 defense candidates.

Housing, feeding, and outfitting crews during the training and trial periods is a big operation and an expensive one. Early in the season, when yachts are doing their preliminary work in home waters, there are few problems. The crews live at home, get themselves to the yacht club or shipyard where their boat is based, and all the owner has to worry about is providing lunch and a few bottles of soda pop.

When the candidates move to Newport for the trial

series, the situation changes abruptly. The crew, super-numeraries, and sometimes wives become charges of the owner. Twelve-Meter yachts have only the sketchiest excuse for living accommodations, so there is no question of the crew making its home on board. Living quarters must be found, meals arranged, and full kits of sailing clothes provided. Until his yacht is eliminated, or, more happily, has completed the defense assignment, the owner must look after the well-being of his people as though he had adopted them as a family. To all intents and purposes he did just that when he brought them together.

Many owners have this in mind; it is obvious in the way they treat their newly acquired responsibilities—they do everything possible to insure their comfort, health, and happiness. Any crew worth its salt responds by giving its utmost to the boat. There is an old military axiom which officers learn early in their careers: "Take care of your men and they'll take care of you when the chips are down." Henry D. Mercer and his *Weatherly* syndicate associates may never have heard this admonition, but they conducted themselves in their crew relations as though they had originated it. So did the *Columbia* syndicate and Captain Matthews in 1958. None could have been more generous in arrangements for the men who sailed, more kind, more thoughtful and considerate. The record shows they were repaid with interest—no morale problems, no questions about the intensity of the competitive effort.

Everyone, as near as possible, lived under the same roof: skipper, brain trust, deck gang. They ate, played, and lived very much as they worked—together—a situation sharply in contrast to that which existed even as late as the thirties. The first J boats (1930) were as devoid of creature comforts as the racing Twelves of today. A couple of pipe berths, two or three heads, a navigator's table, somewhere to stow the lunch—that was about the extent of the furnishings.

So afterguards lived on other yachts, and crews were quartered in houseboats of one form or another. *Enterprise*'s men ate and slept in the hulk of the old and unsuccessful Cup candidate *Corona*, ex-*Colonia*; *Whirlwind*'s, in the 'tween decks of the Maine coasting schooner *Minas Princess*. When the rules were changed to require full living accommodations in Class J sloops, the crews moved on board, lived where they worked.

By the standards of those days, the J boat sailors were much better off than their contemporaries in most forecastles. Their existence, notwithstanding, was Spartan compared to that of their amateur counterparts of two and three decades later. Honcho Heaven, the upper floor of Seafair where *Weatherly*'s bachelors were quartered, would

⚓

To sheet home the jib, two Columbians get that last click on the winch.

have looked like a Waldorf suite to *Weetamoe*'s men, and wearing neckties and jackets to dinner served in an Ocean Drive mansion by uniformed maids was quite beyond their dreams.

"Honcho" may require explanation. Whatever the word's derivation or original meaning, in the Cup boat vernacular of 1962 it meant "one who does the work." Pridefully, winch grinders and sheet handlers, the pulley-hauley boys, reserved the term for themselves and never conferred its distinction on a straw boss or anyone who rode in the cockpit. Honcho Heaven, naturally, was their abode.

The type of group living in vogue among the Cup defense candidates of 1958 and 1962—and the challengers as well—was reminiscent of a boy's school, or that of a large family if wives were part of the establishment. Whatever disadvantages existed for individuals who might occasionally have found it restrictive of their shoreside activities, it certainly had the effect of minimizing, if not eliminating, disciplinary problems and building the kind of team spirit which obviated the mutinies which occurred among earlier Cup crews.

Mutinies in Cup crews? History records three, one of which was so mild in nature that it hardly deserves classification as a rebellion against authority—perhaps it should be called a labor relations misunderstanding. The others, on the other hand, reached the point of a showdown between crew and officers. Authority prevailed in the end.

The first mutiny occurred in July 1901, when *Shamrock II* was being readied for the transatlantic voyage which would bring her to Sandy Hook to race the second *Columbia*. Her crew was offered a bonus of $40.00 above wages for the passage, but fifteen of her sailors refused to sail unless they were paid $75.00 extra for what they described as "going foreign in a bronze bowl." Sir Thomas Lipton's managers promptly fired them and signed on replacements without too much difficulty. Forty dollars was real money at the turn of the century, and there were plenty of mariners ready to work for it.

A somewhat similar situation arose in 1934, when most of *Endeavour*'s deckhands struck for higher wages just before the yacht was to leave for the United States. T. O. M. Sopwith gave the strikers the sack and replaced them with husky young amateurs, who volunteered to sail with *Endeavour*'s nine loyal professionals. The British skipper knew that he was damaging his yacht's chances against *Rainbow* by his action, but he refused to be a holdup victim.

There simply was not enough time left in which to train and condition the newcomers. Professional and amateur alike, the crew worked hard and with a higher degree of efficiency than that which had characterized the performance in the last *Shamrock*, but this mixed crew was no match in speed and precision for *Rainbow*'s well-drilled, horny-handed ensemble.

It is a wonder that *Endeavour* was handled at all toward the end of what developed into a difficult, keenly fought six-race series. After the last race, when the English amateurs came ashore, every man jack of them had hands that looked like raw beef—bleeding, puffed, and blistered. There had not been time to toughen them for the work they had to do. It is a tribute to the courage of these young yachtsmen and a mark of their devotion to the British cause that they heaved and hauled on wet, heavy gear through thirty miles of racing each day.

Few knew about it at the time, but *Rainbow* had a spot of labor trouble—albeit of a formal, dignified kind—just after word of *Endeavour*'s crew trouble reached these shores. The labor-management confrontation in *Rainbow* grew out of a written request for a higher rate of prize money, yachting's traditional incentive pay.

The incident was revealed by C. Sherman Hoyt, writing in his fascinating memoirs:

We were served with a written notice in true "round robin" form; after setting forth their claims, the crew had affixed their signatures radially around a circle. The question was one of prize money. Before the season began, to attain uniformity and to curb at least one form of expense, the managements of all would-be defenders agreed upon a uniform scale of wages and prize money for all hands.

The situation had now changed, and, while obligated by the joint pact, we felt justified in making a slight contingent concession. We refused to alter the scale of prize money, but did compromise to some extent by offering small bonuses to be paid at the end of the season to such as remained in continuous employment, provided we were selected defender and were successful in the final match. Aided by the arguments of our officers and some of the oldest hands, our truly loyal crew accepted. This time they did not sign around a circle, but around a square with a note added: "Now you see we are on the square!"

There were no such incidents when the 12-Meter yachts and amateur yachtsmen came onto the America's Cup scene together. No one was getting paid, anyhow (except a handful of the finest type of professionals), all were housed comfortably, clothed, and fed very well, and everyone was there because he wanted to be. Disciplinary control was exercised gently, and only occasionally was it necessary for a skipper or syndicate manager to make it plain that late-hour social operations of an independent nature were not to interfere in any way with the mission, and that no special privileges could be granted.

A case in point comes to mind. Just before the first meeting of *Gretel* and *Weatherly*, there was a fancy cocktail party to celebrate the Australians' debut in America's Cup circles. Crews of both yachts had been invited, but to no one's surprise both skippers sent regrets on behalf of themselves and all hands. For obvious reasons, with the opening of the series so close at hand, it was hardly the time for America's Cup crews to be milling around on the martini circuit.

One of *Weatherly*'s eligible young bachelors, then courting a lovely little blonde, wanted very much to take her to the party. He asked one of his older shipmates to intercede for him with the skipper, promising that he would be back at Seafair in time for an early turn-in.

The intermediary explained matters to Mosbacher and got this answer: "If X feels that he should go to the party, by all means he should do so. I think it would be only fair to tell him, though, that if he does, he won't be on the boat in the morning." X was at his customary post on *Weatherly* the next day and there has been no sign that his romance was blighted by nonattendance at the cocktail party.

Life at Seafair, at Ocean Manor, the *Columbia* headquarters, at the establishment which the *Nefertiti* crowd affectionately called Mildew Manor, and in the various places where *Easterner*'s men were disposed, was by no means all rigid routine and grim concentration on winning yacht races. Parents and friends came to visit, often remained for dinner. There were invitations to other camps and homes, and like any group of normal young people the sailors had no trouble making their own fun.

Weatherly's crew got a little help in this respect from the Australians, who used to drop around in the evening for a few beers and extemporaneous choral work around the piano. As good hosts, the men of *Weatherly* entered into the spirit of the Aussie visits until they began to

suspect that they were being double-teamed, that the *Gretel* organization was divided into a sailing crew and one devoted to the lighter side of life. This suspicion grew out of their observation that the men working on *Gretel*'s deck the next day rarely were those who had kept them up the night before.

Every crew had its light-hearted, quick-witted members who kept dullness a cable's length away. *Weatherly* had two effervescent comedians, Charley Bertrand and Bizzy Monte-Sano, and in Don Browning, a quieter, somewhat more dignified dispenser of the right word at the right time.

There was objectivity in their humor, too. One morning when there was to be no race, but a practice session had been scheduled, the weather was nasty. It was blowing raw and hard from the east, there was rain in the air, and the seas breaking into foam on the rocks in front of Seafair were ugly. Sailing would have been no fun at all,

⚓

"Knapp's railbirds" was the nickname bestowed on Weatherly's *crew in 1958, and this picture shows why.* Weatherly *was tender that season, had a tendency to heel too much in a good breeze, so Skipper Arthur Knapp (a* Ranger *afterguardsman 21 years earlier) used to make all hands drape themselves over the weather rail where their weight would do the most good when he was working the yacht to windward.*

so *Weatherly*'s crew, hoping for a day off, took its own steps to insure that the severity of the weather was not lost on Skipper Mosbacher, who was having, for once, a leisurely breakfast.

His attention was drawn from the morning newspaper by the thrashing of wind-tortured shrubs against the dining room windows and the ominous, persistent moaning of half a gale through an adjoining hall. Mosbacher, thoroughly familiar with the virtuosity of his associates, crossed stealthily to the hall door and flung it open. There stood Monte-Sano leading his shipmates in synthetic wind sounds while outside Bertrand provided the visual effects by creating turbulence among the bushes.

Mosbacher laughed at Monte-Sano's now sheepish chorus and then evoked a cheer by saying: "Okay, men. I'm convinced. No sailing today." Everyone piled into automobiles and drove to the Newport Y.M.C.A. to play basketball under the leadership of Bob Gibson, who had been a varsity star in the sport at the University of Rhode Island.

Things were somewhat different in the thirties, when there was little if any contact between crew and afterguard when the day's sail ended. The men got regular liberty, and it was up to the sailing master and his mates to see that they were in shape to perform their duties the next day. Those who were not were soon on the beach, job hunting.

Afterguards usually numbered five and lived together on yachts moored in Brenton Cove. They spent their evenings playing cards, reading, or doing what sailors everywhere usually do when together—talk about boats. Once in a while there was a dinner party on another yacht or ashore. One of the more notable of these was given by the yachting writers for the afterguards of *Enterprise* and *Endeavour* in an extremely respectable dining room.

It was, of course, the time of prohibition in the U.S.A., but the resourceful journalists had contrived to provide liquids calculated to remove any stiffness or stuffiness which would spoil the occasion. It was a very gay, relaxed evening, and when it ended late strollers were treated to the spectacle of a distinguished British designer perched perilously on the roof of a sedan being driven through Newport's narrow hill streets by an equally distinguished writer, whose steering vision was obscured by the flapping overcoat worn by a famous American naval architect sitting astride the motor hood.

No one fell off the conveyance, nor did the automobile hit anything on its way to the New York Yacht Club land-

In the second race of the 1962 series, sailed in a 20-knot wind, Gretel *hammers her way to windward with lee rail down and water flying all over. Sturrock and his navigator are interested in something astern.*

ing to deliver its passengers to waiting launches. This incident ranks among the miracles in America's Cup annals, especially considering that the driver was completely unaware that there was someone on his car roof.

When one of the *Columbia* or *Weatherly* and *Nefertiti* crew members craved a change of evening scenery, all he had to do was step into the driveway, get into a car, and go. The *Easterner*'s crew merely stepped off *Rover*'s deck onto the Newport Shipyard pier and were on their way.

It was neither that easy nor convenient in the days of C. Sherman Hoyt. When he was a member of *Rainbow*'s afterguard, he lived on board the motor yacht *Vara* with Commodore Vanderbilt. As far as *Rainbow*'s skipper was concerned, this was an excellent arrangement for it enabled him to keep an eye on his gregarious, convivial aide, and to turn in at night secure in the knowledge that Sherman too would soon be in his bunk, safe from the temptations of the Muenchinger-King's Victorian retreat for thirsty yachtsmen, or the less attractive oases on Thames Street.

He was not—not always, at any rate. Small doses of the quiet life on *Vara* sufficed for Sherman. There were times when he felt the need to stretch his legs ashore, and perchance have a noggin or two of cheer if he fell in with a kindred spirit. To facilitate these digressions, *Rainbow*'s co-helmsman had had the foresight to arrange privately with one of *Vara*'s seamen to keep his frostbite sailing dinghy, *Ma Winterbottom*, rigged and ready for use after dark at the port (crew's) gangway.

So, when the shore lights beckoned after Vanderbilt had retired to his cabin and the starboard gangway was secured, Sherman quietly descended the ladder to his dinghy and sailed through the darkness to a convenient Thames Street landing. Some hours later solicitous friends would escort Sherman back to *Ma Winterbottom*, cast off the painter, and shove the dinghy and Sherman in the general direction of *Vara*. It is a tribute to Hoyt's sailing genius that he never failed to make it back to the ship where his faithful, if somewhat sleepy, collaborator waited at the gangway to spirit him back aboard.

It is not likely that these absences without leave always escaped Vanderbilt's notice, but the Commodore never let Sherman know that he was aware of them. He would not have wanted to spoil his fun.

MATCH RACE TACTICS

Where Mistakes Hurt Most

"When leading, stay between your opponent and the next mark" is the axiomatic foundation on which the tactical structure of match racing is erected. Boat-for-boat contests, which often take on the aspects of man-to-man combat, have very little in common with the more prevalent fleet racing engaged in by one-design classes, or distance racers competing on handicap.

The maxim is as sound as it is simple, but there are countless skippers who regretfully remember races they lost because, through aberration, misplaced confidence in the capabilities of their boats, or just plain negligence, they failed to cover a rival who split tacks or jibes with them. Usually the penalty is devastatingly final—defeat.

As with most rules, however, there are situations that cry for exceptions. Knowing when to invoke them instead of following doctrine is the badge of the successful match racer.

It requires courage and profound faith in one's racing judgment to ignore the book when an adversary, tucked under your lee, tacks away when your boat is laying the windward mark. Do you come about with him, or do you display your independence by holding on for the buoy?

Does your opponent know or see something that you do not, or is he merely trying to lure you into overstanding, a mishap which can only reduce your lead? If you continue on course and fetch the mark, your lead will grow in direct ratio to the time and distance lost by your opponent through his extra tack. If you fail to make the mark, either through miscalculation or an unlucky wind shift, you're the goat. Conversely, your adversary will glow with the brilliance of genius for having had the foresight to make the tack that enabled him to fetch the turning mark which you missed.

When an America's Cup defense candidate is faced with this situation, much more is involved in the decision to tack or not to tack than the uninitiated can imagine. Cup-racing tactics are influenced by such diverse factors as human psychology, weather, predetermined strategy, sails, weaknesses and strengths of the protagonists, and, to some degree, even public relations.

Emil (Bus) Mosbacher, Jr., who sailed *Weatherly* to a hard-won victory over Australia's *Gretel* in 1962, sums it up in these somewhat cynical words: "So much of what you do is not so much what you think you *should* do in the circumstances as it is what you think the educated observers *think* you should do."

Before the wise skipper makes a tactical decision in a Cup trial match, Bus believes, he must give some thought to the probable reactions of these educated observers (second guessers)—members of the selection committee, of course, then yachting writers, and the more knowing of the onlookers. All are, by the very nature of the sport in which they are involved, second guessers, deep dyed.

There is an old saw that goes: "There are two things in this life which most people are sure they can do better than the person who by training and experience and skill is qualified to do. One is to run a newspaper, the other to manage a baseball team." After more than thirty years on the yacht-racing circuit, I feel strongly that a third item should be added: sail a racing yacht.

Bus would agree, I think. "You must keep in mind the fact," he warns, "that it is always possible for a spectator to sail your boat better from his point of vantage than you can do it yourself from the cockpit right in the thick of things. Or he thinks he can, which amounts to the same thing. No one ever makes a mistake sailing another's race."

Therefore, Mosbacher points out, it is sometimes necessary to consider how a maneuver will look to potential critics as well as how it will affect the tactical situation.

It is obviously essential that the man seeking the honor of being chosen to sail an America's Cup defender make the right impression on the selection committee. Besides demonstrating that as a helmsman he can get the most out of his boat, he must instill in the selectors confidence that he can be depended upon to make what they consider the proper move at the right time in any tactical crisis.

Of less importance, granted, is what newspaper and magazine pundits and sailing enthusiasts think of his racing acumen, but it must be borne in mind that the New York Yacht Club America's Cup committee members do read press accounts of trial races, and they cannot always shut their ears to clubmates' opinions on a subject in which they have a deep mutual interest.

It is no reflection on the competence, judgment, and integrity of these men to say that they would be less than

⚓

Both yachts are going for the weather end of the line on the starboard tack. Endeavour II (*dark hull*) *is holding high to prevent* Ranger *from getting an overlap to windward which, under the international rules then in force, would have entitled her to room at the buoy after the starting signal.*

Endeavour II, *obviously a little early and unwilling to bear away down the line and give* Ranger *the windward berth, sails herself to the wrong side of the starting buoy, forcing herself to tack, wear ship, and then head for the line. Meanwhile, Vanderbilt, timing his moves exactly, has wiped* Ranger *off under the British yacht's stern, and is going for the line. The buoy marking the weather end of the line can just be seen to leeward of* Endeavour's *port counter and the end of her boom.*

The result. A few minutes later Ranger *is right where she wanted to be—sitting comfortably to windward of* Endeavour's *bow. (The quadrilateral or "Greta Garbo" jibs set on both yachts are no longer legal.)*

human if what they read and heard from other observers of the yachting scene did not to some extent color their thinking about what they had seen with their own eyes.

Let us take a not uncommon situation in match racing. Boat A has the weather gauge on Boat B and is laying the windward mark. Boat B tacks away from the leader. Does Boat A adhere strictly to the fundamental stay-between-your-opponent-and-the-next-mark rule, or does she hold her course, fetch the mark, and gain distance while her opponent is covering unnecessary ground?

How will the selection committee react? What will its view of the problem be? Will its members regard Boat A's skipper as a dull, textbook sailor, or give him full marks for tactical soundness, if he does the conventional thing and tacks with his opponent? Will they condemn him as reckless and unreliable, or applaud him as a man of cool, discerning judgment, if he does not follow Boat B into a maneuver which can only benefit Boat B unless a wind shift favors the new tack?

What will the spectators say over their post-race cocktails? What will the newspapers report the next morning? If you think that baseball writers and bleacherites are accomplished hindsighters when passing judgment on a Casey Stengel decision to go for the hit-and-run play instead of the sacrifice bunt, you should hear what yachtsmen say about skippers whose most soundly conceived tactics do not produce the looked-for result. The opening words of virtually every sentence they utter are: "He should have . . ."

Good judgment and unflagging faith in his ability to exercise it are attributes of winning helmsmen as well as dugout masterminds, and the chances are they pay off at least as often for the sailor as they do for the ball player.

Mosbacher, troubled about the advisability of always covering an adversary, once discussed it with Commodore Harold S. Vanderbilt, kingpin of the J boat era in America's Cup history. "If you are pretty sure you are on the lay line for the weather mark," he asked, "do you follow if your opponent tacks away?"

Vanderbilt's answer was a firm, "No."

It is quite likely that Bus had this in mind in the last race of the 1962 observation series, when *Weatherly* was matched with *Nefertiti* for the fourth time. Because Mosbacher outmaneuvered the new Marblehead boat, he put *Weatherly* in the weather berth at the start and kept her there on the beat up a good sou'wester toward the Point Judith whistle buoy, the first turning mark on the course.

Half a mile from the buoy, perhaps a little more, Ted Hood put *Nefertiti* about to get out of *Weatherly*'s backwind. Mosbacher, noting that *Weatherly* was laying the mark, held the starboard tack, and let Hood go inshore 150 yards on the port tack by himself.

Outside the shelter of the Point, the seas were larger and

the foul tide stronger. Their combined effect knocked *Weatherly* down just enough to make her miss the mark by not more than half a length. There was too much sea and tide to try to "shoot" the buoy so *Weatherly* had to make two little hitches to get around. While she was thus engaged, *Nefertiti* came up from a position somewhat to windward, moving with a rap full. She drove inside of *Weatherly* at the turn before Mosbacher would fill away on his rounding tack. *Weatherly* eventually lost that race and the second guessers were in full voice that night in Newport.

"Mosbacher should have gone with Hood; never let him go. He should have stayed between him and the mark. If he had done so, he would have held his lead." This was the theme of the chorus.

Now let's hear what Mosbacher has to say about the incident.

The forecast was for the wind to increase in velocity in the afternoon and we knew that *Nefertiti* was very fast under her huge spinnaker in a good breeze and she had been going very well to windward when it blew strongly. Therefore we felt that we had to build up as much of a lead as possible on the first windward leg before the breeze piped up so that we could hold her on the long run down to the lee mark at Schuyler Ledge and start the beat back to the finish in a position to keep on her wind.

When Teddy took that last tack in toward Point Jude we let him go because we were laying the mark. If we fetched, we would increase our lead over *Nefertiti* by the amount of time and distance Ted used in making his clearing tack and coming about to lay the mark. That would put us in a good position from which to sail the rest of the race.

Well, you know what happened. Beyond the Point the seas were rougher and the tide was running stronger on our weather bow than we had expected. We just didn't quite make it—about six feet at a guess—and we didn't dare to try to luff around in that slop. We had to take two short hitches to get around and Ted, who had actually overstood a little, came roaring right through us at the buoy. That changed the whole picture, but I think that if I had to do it again I would do the same thing. It puts you on a spot, though, when you don't make what everyone thinks is the indicated covering tack. What you do has to turn out exactly right or you are wide open to criticism.

Three days earlier in the same waters and in an almost identical situation, *Weatherly* had broken *Nefertiti*'s five-race winning streak by doing the identical thing—letting *Nefertiti* go and holding on for the mark.

A mile from Point Judith whistler, *Nefertiti*, down in *Weatherly*'s lee, tacked offshore. Mosbacher let Hood go rather than run the risk of overstanding the weather mark by going out with him. The decision paid big dividends. *Weatherly* came in just short enough of the mark to give her crew time to get set up on the fetching tack for the rounding and spinnaker set. The maneuver was executed efficiently and *Weatherly* was off and winging while *Nefertiti* was still sailing for the buoy.

99

Because what happened in the first of these pictures happened when it did, you see Weatherly in the second picture leading Gretel to the finish of the closest race in America's Cup history, the fourth of the 1962 series. The Defender's victory margin was only 26 seconds in a fresh breeze, about 3½ boat lengths in distance.

Halfway down the final leg on which Gretel (nearer camera) had been gaining, the wind shifted from the yachts' port quarter to abeam. Weatherly promptly set her reacher and took in her spinnaker. Gretel held onto her kite a little longer, sagging off to leeward of the course in order to do so, and then followed suit. Weatherly regained some of her lost ground as the rivals reached toward the finish. Then, when the wind swung aft again and the Australian rushed back into contention, the defender's crew made its fastest and most perfect spinnaker set.

This is the way they finished after Sturrock had made several attempts from his leeward position to sail Gretel up across Weatherly's stern and onto her wind. He was repulsed each time and finally had to fall off and go for the line. No loser ever had made it this close.

Nefertiti, having made quite a long board on the offshore tack, came in closer to the mark, but obviously had lost some distance to *Weatherly* after splitting tacks. The pressure was now on the big white yacht to make up that ground. Her crew hurried the spinnaker set, and botched the job so badly that the acre of nylon which *Nefertiti* had forward of her mast went up with more twists in it than a cruller. The crew fought to unwind them, but only made things worse. Eventually the whole wriggling, flailing mass had to be brought down to the deck, thrown below, and replaced by another kite. *Weatherly* won that race going away, and the records of the Cup match with *Gretel* show that on three occasions the defender increased her margin over the challenger by not covering when the Australian took a tack which caused her to overstand the weather mark.

It is possible to argue the stay-between-the-mark-and-your-opponent maxim from both sides. There is a time for doing so just as there is an equally good time for not doing it. The history of the 1962 observation trials at Newport reveals, however, that more races were lost by disobeying the rule than by observing it; far more.

Mosbacher lost a comfortable lead in one race by not covering a badly beaten opponent, regained the initiative by superior windward work, lost it again by too strict adherence to the covering doctrine, and finally won the race because his opponent ignored it.

There were all manner of lessons to be learned from this extremely exciting see-saw on the familiar windward-leeward course from one of the torpedo range buoys in the approaches to Narragansett Bay out to Point Judith whistler and return, twice around.

On the second turn to windward, *Weatherly* was far ahead of *Columbia*, which had put herself deep in a hole in the early stages of the race by falling off the wind to go around a fish trap running perpendicular to the shore, while *Weatherly* was sailing boldly through a narrow passage between the nets and their outermost buoys.

Steadily losing ground to Mosbacher, Shields had to do something different. He put *Columbia* about onto the port tack and stood in toward the Narragansett shore. At that moment, *Weatherly*, a good quarter of a mile ahead, sailed into what the British call a "luffing puff," but what generally is known in American sailing patois as a "lift," that is, a slant of breeze which lifts the recipient closer to the windward side of the course. It is, of course, a lift if you happen to be on the right tack; it is a header, a force which drives you away from the mark, if you are on the other.

Since this was a starboard tack lift and a good one, Mosbacher chose to profit thereby instead of taking the header he would get by following Shields onto the port tack before the shift petered out. When Mosbacher had extracted the fullest benefit from the lift he came about and was astonished to see that Shields, who by this time was well inshore of his position, had tacked under the beach into a breeze which was not only lifting *Columbia* a couple of points but was much stronger than the air offshore.

Shields appeared to be sailing right around *Weatherly*'s bow. At the worst, he was cutting his deficit rapidly. As the yachts converged, it was touch and go whether *Columbia* would cross the boat she had been chasing all afternoon. We shall never know because, as the moment of truth neared, *Weatherly*'s jib halyard shackle let go and her headsail slid down the stay. By the time it was reset on the spare halyard, *Columbia* had assumed the lead.

She could not hold it, though. It took Mosbacher exactly two fairly short tacks to re-establish himself as the leader. Subsequent tactics indicated that once having been bitten, Mosbacher was twice shy. Every time *Columbia* tried to split tacks, *Weatherly* was put about right on top of her. Whether it was slavish adherence to the covering rule, or less than precise navigation in the light fog outside of Point Judith, is a matter of opinion, but the fact remains that *Weatherly* overstood the mark much more than did *Columbia* and thus rounded astern of her, a second loss of lead.

So once again the demonstrably faster yacht was in the trailing berth as the boats began a spinnaker run home. Halfway to the finish, the breeze began to haul out of the southwest toward north; wind conditions inside the long finger of land pointing offshore to Block Island were different than they were outside. Down came the big kites, up went genoa jibs and the boats reached on the port tack with sheets just lifted.

Mosbacher held *Weatherly* high of the course, working up into the breeze. Shields kept *Columbia* on the rhumb line to the finish. He did not sharpen up to *Weatherly*'s course to keep between her and the committee boat. Because he violated the match racer's first commandment, he lost the race.

Weatherly came down from the windward side of the course with a bone in her teeth, moving four feet to *Columbia*'s three. She sailed right past *Columbia* to weather without meeting the expected challenging luff. *Weatherly* preceded *Columbia* over the finish line by a length of open water.

Columbia had been given two opportunities to win a race in which she had been widely outsailed to windward when the boats were in the same water. She threw away the second and critical one simply by not staying between a beaten opponent and the next mark. It was another bitter lesson for young Shields, new to the tensions of Cup trial competition; a lesson, by the way, he had difficulty absorbing. He lost two other trial tests which he should have won only because he failed to keep *Columbia* between her adversary and the finish on the course's last off-wind leg.

In her defense of the Cup against Sceptre in 1958, Columbia *was always ready for the next move. Here she is reaching under spinnaker with the pole well forward, the jib hoisted in stops on the stay ready to break out at the next mark and another spinnaker going aloft in stops to windward of the one already set. When the replacement for it is broken out and drawing, the original kite will come down easily behind it and the change will have been made so smoothly that most of the spectators will not have noticed the shift.*

Sceptre *may not have been a fast boat, but she had an unmatched wardrobe of finery of which this vast Herbulot nylon spinnaker was a sample.* Sceptre's *kites were big and beautiful, but not nearly so effective as* Columbia's *smaller but more efficiently cut spinnakers.*

In the fourth race of the observation series he had taken the lead from *Nefertiti* in a light-air race by tacking downwind, a tactic which put the 1958 defender three lengths ahead of the somewhat ponderous Marblehead yacht with half of the last leg to sail. *Nefertiti,* notoriously slow when dead before a soft breeze, decided to see what downwind tacking could do for her. She swung over to the port jibe and held up to the easterly side of the base course. *Columbia,* instead of jibing inside of her, kept her main boom on the port side and her spinnaker full to starboard.

A few minutes later, when the boats were widely separated laterally, the breeze swung into the southeast, freshened to fifteen knots and, because she was out there, hit *Nefertiti* first. Before the new breeze got down to *Columbia,* *Nefertiti* was on her fastest point of sailing, broad reaching in a fresh breeze. She moved with the alacrity of a scalded cat, sailed right around *Columbia,* and won by half a mile.

"Lucky *Nefertiti,*" you say? To a degree, perhaps, but she did what the trailing boat normally is committed to doing—something different from the leader. That is, of course, if the leader allows her to do so. This *Columbia* did. Luck never entered the situation until sound judgment slumbered on *Columbia.* To protect her hard-won lead, *Columbia* should have been on the same jibe, on the same side of the course as her adversary—between her and the next mark, in this case the finish.

Exactly a week later, *Columbia* handed *Nefertiti* another race by making the same mistake. The slippery gray boat from Long Island Sound had carried a 54-second lead onto the final nine-mile genoa jib reach to the finish of a triangular race. On the homeward leg, though, *Columbia* steered a higher course than *Nefertiti,* which appeared to be on the rhumb line.

Observers (second guessers if you will) expected *Columbia,* even though she believed her course to be right and *Nefertiti*'s wrong, to come down to her opponent's line, and thus put herself between the big white boat and the finish. She did not. She held high. *Nefertiti* sailed right through her lee and won by 24 seconds, something she could not have done had *Columbia* been where she belonged—between the Marbleheader and whatever part of the finish line she was heading for.

Nefertiti, by all odds the recipient of more gifts in the observation series than any other candidate that year, won another race because no less a skilled, seasoned racing helmsman than Ray Hunt let a beaten boat go about her business unattended on the reaching leg to the finish.

Don McNamara was steering *Nefertiti* that day. Unable to break through *Easterner* or make any dent on her lead in the first two miles, Don took the white boat high of the course. Hunt let him go and gave *Easterner* her head for the barn. To those familiar with the waters, Hunt's reasoning was plain and solidly based. Under the existing conditions, as the yachts neared the Narragansett shore on the port tack they could expect to be headed. When this happened the boat to windward of the other's track and astern could expect to be knocked down into the leader's wake and thus irrevocably beaten.

That day, the constant was inconstant; things did not work out according to the established pattern. The heading process was gradual, almost imperceptible, and it was selective. It slowly knocked *Easterner* down until she could not quite lay the finish line, but it ignored *Nefertiti*. McNamara's boat, in more stable and perhaps slightly stronger breeze out to the eastward, came down on *Easterner* with sheets cracked, traveling like a racing sports car on a straightaway. Soon she was overlapped on *Easterner*'s windward side and eating past her. Hunt luffed, but too late. *Nefertiti*, instead of luffing with *Easterner*, rolled right through the wind onto the other tack and headed for the line. When *Easterner* fell off on the starboard tack she was a length in *Nefertiti*'s wake. That was the ball game. An instant later *Nefertiti* got the winner's gun. *Easterner* followed her over the line by 11 seconds.

It is characteristic of the "stay-between" rule that there always seem to be perfectly logical reasons for departing from it in what one of the principals decides is a special situation. It is just as characteristic of the rule that its violators are punished by having victory snatched from their grasp.

Attacking as well as defensive patterns must vary according to one skipper's estimate of the other's competitive capabilities. According to Bus Mosbacher:

Something you would try on one opponent you would be wasting your time attempting with someone else. Knowing your opponent's racing philosophy and how he will react to a given set of circumstances are of inestimable value in match racing. That is why the first race or two of a Cup series are very much like the opening rounds of a prize fight—the principals are feeling each other out, probing for weaknesses.

It is a great help to know, for instance, that if you tack the other fellow will follow automatically, and as rapidly as he can execute the maneuver. Such a skipper, by his eagerness to cover, sets himself up for a false tack, or double tack if you will, which would open the door for escape into clean air. It is always wise, I think, not to be impetuous about tacking with an opponent who is trying to break away; better be sure that the other boat commits herself to going about before you follow, especially if you suspect that her skipper is likely to try the false tack trick.

At any rate, it is always a good idea to have plenty of way on your boat when starting a covering tack so that if your adversary rolls back to the tack on which he was sailing before he initiated his fake, you can do the same with minimum sacrifice of boat speed and no loss of distance to the other fellow. Alertness is the key in this situation, that and close observation of what actually is going on in the other boat, not what the enemy wants you to *think* is happening.

Columbia *tacking ship. Just before the evolution. Navigator Stephens takes a bearing from the port compass, Shields steadies the wheel, and the crew relaxes.*

"Ready about!" At the helmsman's command, the crew goes to assigned tacking stations.

Coming through the wind's eye now, Columbia's boom swings across the deck and the cockpit hands are casting off what is becoming the leeward backstay and setting up the windward runner.

While Columbia gathers way on the port tack, winch grinders on the lee side sheet the jib in flat and the two cockpit men combine forces to get the weather backstay set at the proper tension. Time for the maneuver—from full on one tack to full on the other—7 or 8 seconds in a moderate breeze, 12 to 15 in heavy.

It became evident to Mosbacher and his afterguard during the *Gretel-Weatherly* match that the defender was the faster, closer-winded boat working to weather, and that *Gretel* stayed closest to the American yacht when she engaged her in prolonged short-tacking duels. When they settled down on the inevitable long board to the windward mark after having short-tacked along one side of the course, *Weatherly* always sailed away from the Australian.

Therefore it was equally plain to the *Weatherly* brain trust that Jock Sturrock's best gambit was to keep tacking to make *Weatherly* match *Gretel* tack for tack. Bus said in assessing the situation:

That was one of Jock's greatest strengths. He had a bigger, stronger crew than ours—no better in skills and attitude, certainly, but physically superior—and the mechanical advantage of the linked winches which made it possible for four pumpers to work one drum at the same time and thus sheet home the genoa jib faster than we could.

Naturally, because he was always behind on the windward legs, Jock played the game which he could play best, hoping to force us into a foul-up which would change the entire picture. We played it with him until the fifth race.

Before that one I talked the situation over with George [O'Day], Bob [Bus' younger brother and former North American men's champion] and Mr. Mercer. We all felt that we were only playing into the Australians' hands by short tacking with them when we could outsail them to windward and, since we had a 3-to-1 lead in the series we could afford to try something different.

We therefore agreed that if we got ahead of *Gretel* on the windward leg we would put on a loose cover rather than a tight one—just stay generally between her and the mark and on her starboard side for tacking purposes instead of following her tack for tack and trying to keep right on her wind.

We knew when we made the decision that we would have to live with it. You saw how well it worked. We beat him comfortably the first time up wind and put him another minute and eleven seconds farther astern the second time. Our strategy worked out perfectly. Can you imagine the howl that would have gone up if it hadn't? Wow!

The importance of winning the start in a match race is difficult to overemphasize. Position is the controlling factor here, not time. It is of no importance whether a boat crosses the line a split second or five minutes after the go signal so long as she is where she wants to be with relation to her opponent. This may be right under her lee bow in the case of a boat which can look the wind in the eye and go where she is looking. It can to be windward and ahead. And it can be off by herself at the opposite end of the line. It all depends on where a skipper has decided beforehand that he wants to put his boat and, of course, whether the opponent will cooperate by not upsetting the plan.

We are assuming here that the start is to windward; it always has been in the recent America's Cup matches and in the trials which produce the New York Yacht Club's defender.

All manner of elements enter into the planning of a start. The relative capabilities of the boats under the existing wind conditions, the length of the starting line and its angle to the wind, and which side of the course to windward a skipper wishes to favor because of tidal current conditions or an expected wind shift are some of the factors which the thoughtful tactician takes into account.

Bus Mosbacher, who in 1958 invented the pre-start maneuver which made two boats look like one dog chasing its tail, used it most effectively in the trials of that year when he was at *Vim*'s wheel, but only rarely four years later when he was in *Weatherly*. This tactic calls for one boat in the pre-start period to put its bow almost on the transom of her opponent when the latter is heading away from the line and thereafter maintain such a position that the pursued can neither jibe nor tack without fouling the pursuer. Thus the trailing boat keeps the other from going for the starting line until she herself breaks off the chase and goes first.

"The best spot for this chasing tactic is off the end of the starting line," Bus says, "so that when the pursuer decides the time is ripe to head for the line he is reaching for it and the enemy cannot get on his wind, thus spoiling the whole effort."

He explained:

This tail-chasing maneuver was really conceived as a defensive measure to help a slower boat to protect herself against a faster opponent. In *Vim*, though, it became an offensive weapon because we had a better crew than any of the other boats at that time except *Weatherly*, and we could out-boat handle the opposition. It is rather an effective method of probing for weaknesses in the other fellow, too, and it used to have certain psychological advantages.

In 1958, remember, the average sailing time of the starting line was one minute. In 1962, for some reason, it was lengthened to three minutes. Therefore position on the line became more important than the chasing maneuver which no longer had the element of surprise anyway.

This last time around, we tried at the start to be in a position which made it possible to go where we wanted to go, provided Jock would let us. He was a real fine competitor and certainly didn't make things easy for us. Generally, though, we were able to carry out our plans. These were based on wind direction and velocity, whether it was steady or likely to shift, which way the tide was running and how strongly.

Take the third race of our match with *Gretel* as an example, the one in which the boats started at opposite ends of the line. It must have looked strange to the spectators, but there was a reason for it. According to the official club records, *Weatherly* started 63 seconds after *Gretel* crossed the line, but what the records do not show is that we were pretty much where we wanted to be and when we wanted to be.

If you remember that race, both of us were to windward of the line after the preparatory signal, jilling around with-

The command has been given: "Stand by to jibe!" All hands are at jibing stations.

Columbia *jibing ship while running dead before the wind. She used the pole dipping method with twin afterguys worked out on* Vim *in 1958 and now in general use.*

The operation begins. Jack Webb eases the lift to let the spinnaker pole end come down to the deck. Palmer Sparkman, in bow facing aft, clears the "lazy" or non-working wire afterguy to make it ready for use. Dick Ronan, back to camera, heaves in on pole downhaul, or forward guy, as Webb eases lift.

Now the spinnaker has been released from the pole and is flying free as the pole is being swung forward where Sparkman will guide it inside the jibstay. Aft, the mainsail is being hauled in.

The spinnaker pole has been swung through to the port side and the bow man is clipping the afterguy into the fitting on the outboard end. As soon as this is done, the guy is wound in by winch to bring the pole's end and spinnaker clew together.

Cockpit crew now goes into action. As helmsman spins wheel to port, the backstay man (Olin Stephens) lets starboard backstay go and begins to set up port runner and his partner hauls in the mainsheet.

Jibe-O! The boom swings across the boat as the winchman amidships winds in the spinnaker pole afterguy to bring the pole aft.

On the new jibe, Columbia's crew is hard at work to finish the job smoothly. The pole is being squared and Ronan has left the foredeck to trim the spinnaker sheet from the starboard winch.

All squared away on the port jibe. Nothing is left to do except make final adjustments in set of the spinnaker, and coil all those lines lying about the deck. It took a long time to describe this evolution, but Columbia's crew needed only about 10 seconds to execute it. Going from wide on one jibe to wide on the other is easiest and quickest; jibing from reach to reach in strong breezes takes twice as long.

out jibs. Some seconds before the gun we squared away and ran back toward about the middle of the line on the starboard jibe with *Gretel* right astern of us on the same jibe. When we got to the line we broke out our jib, sheeted in the main and headed on the starboard tack for the buoy end of the line. We felt that end was markedly favored and anyhow we wanted to be on that side of the course because we had a feeling that any shift in the breeze would favor that side.

When we flattened our sheets, *Gretel* went to leeward of us, jibed, broke out her jib and started on the port tack near the committee boat. When we got to the buoy we went over to the port tack and just about this time *Gretel* came about onto starboard. As we converged it looked as though we were going to cross her, but we got a little header and had to go under Jock's stern. *Gretel* soon tacked to windward of our course so there we were, four minutes after the start, abeam of each other with *Weatherly* beginning to go through *Gretel*.

If *Gretel* had not tacked when she did, we would have gone out on the port tack until we could have come about on her weather quarter. Then, if we had been headed, we could tack again and be on the inside of any subsequent shift favoring that side of the course. We didn't have to do this because when *Gretel* tacked we had our wind clear and were able to work up across her into what we had decided beforehand was the right geographical position on the course. As things turned out, the wind did shift northerly as we expected it might, but not until we were so far to windward of *Gretel* that we overstood the first mark somewhat. We had such a good position, though, that we weren't hurt too much.

Charley Barr, Cup hero of the turn-of-the-century period, was a sailing master who believed devoutly in the value of position at the start and, historians of the sport tell us, rarely allowed yachting ethics to hamper his maneuvering. What he did in the 1901 trials to *Constitution*, which Nat Herreshoff had hailed as the fastest boat he ever designed and one which would defeat *Columbia* easily, illustrates how priceless is the knowledge of one's match race opponent and his weaknesses.

Barr knew his professional vis-à-vis, Captain Rhodes, very well; knew that he could be bluffed, that he could be sailed into unhappy situations, because his owners had so deeply impressed upon him the necessity for caution that he would not insist on his rights under the rules in close quarters. Barr sailed accordingly.

Thomas W. Lawson wrote in *The Lawson History of the America's Cup* after *Columbia*'s selection to meet the second *Shamrock*:

In starts *Constitution* was undoubtedly sailed with marked timidity, almost invariably receiving the crumbs after *Columbia* made off with the loaf. Captain Barr, in *Columbia*, had his vessel under perfect control at all times and, with a touch of Scotch canniness, generally put her where he wanted her to be without special regard for the niceties of the rights of others so long as those rights were not insisted upon.

If Captain Rhodes erred more in one direction than

116

another, it was in lack of spirit in obeying orders to dodge *Columbia* in starts at any cost. Some skippers would have insisted on following their own judgment, even at the expense of their position. Captain Rhodes carried out his orders to the detriment of his reputation as a sailing master and came in for some extremely sharp criticism.

The sharpest criticism, perhaps, was delivered by the most trenchant yachting critic of those times, Thomas Fleming Day, the outspoken, crusading editor of *Rudder* magazine. He wore no kid gloves when he went to work on Barr, Rhodes, and the latter's syndicate of employers.

In an article on the final trials he said:

Barr simply made a monkey of the other man. He forced him to do whatever he wished and shoved and jostled *Constitution*, the latter's skipper giving way in the most complaisant manner. The *Constitution* crowd seemed to be deathly afraid of Barr, and whenever it came to a close question their only anxiety seemed to be to get out of the way and give him all the rope he wanted. Their excuse for this cringing was that they did not want to have their boat injured; a most childish excuse, and one that no experienced man would make. Barr is no fool, and if he found he was up against a man with stiff backbone not only would he not try to force such a game, but he would know when his share of the rush had reached its limit and give way in time to save any trouble. . . .

At the start of the third day of trial races, Barr violated all rules of civilized warfare. He simply drove Rhodes off the line and onto the wrong side of the committee boat.

. . . Barr two or three times bore down on *Constitution* when there was no necessity for it, his object being to prevent her from drawing ahead, clearing her wind and tacking. He deliberately established an overlap so as to prevent her going on the other board and held it until it was no longer possible for Rhodes to clear the lee mark boat. He then took the line, leaving *Constitution* to wear around and be handicapped.

Charley Barr was fortunate to have been sailing Cup boats sixty years ago, not now. Race committees and America's Cup committees must have been cut from a different pattern in the early days of this century than that which came into vogue in the thirties and is still fashionable. No matter how timid the tiger at the other tiller, it is impossible to conceive of present-day officials allowing the little Scotsman to roughhouse an opponent as he did Rhodes and *Constitution*.

He may have gotten away with it once, but the next time he tried it the Cup committee would, in a very nice but equally firm way, have laid him out in spades. It would have been made clear to him that what he was doing to the opposition before the start was not the purpose of the exercise; that he would execute his tactical designs within the framework of the racing rules, or else. The committee does not look with favor upon timidity, lack of imagination, and initiative on the part of skippers seeking to defend the Cup; nor can it condone the slurring

Nefertiti *overtaking and passing* Columbia *to windward on a broad reach under spinnaker.*

A few minutes later. Nefertiti *has established herself nicely to windward of Columbia, despite the latter's belated decision to sail higher.*

Here comes Nefertiti (striped spinnaker) on her favorite point of sailing, reaching with spinnaker forward. Her bow wave indicates speed at which she is moving through the water. It looks as though there is still time for Columbia to sharpen up to keep between Nefertiti and the finish.

Any minute now Nefertiti *will reach the position where her expanse of sail will blanket* Columbia.

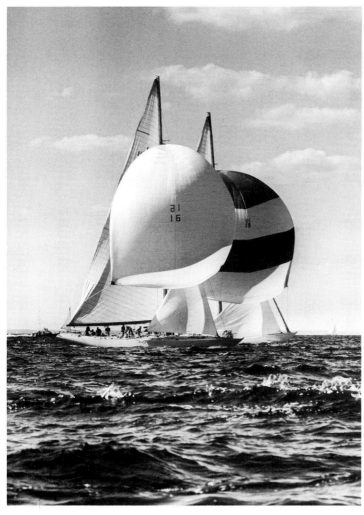

Columbia *breaks off her luff and squares away as* Nefertiti's *greater speed carries her past, well to windward.*

Under Nefertiti's *blanket,* Columbia's *spinnaker collapses. While the gray boat's crew fights to get the kite filled again,* Nefertiti *storms past on her way to victory.*

of ethics and cavalier treatment of yachting's canons of sportsmanship.

Generally speaking, the initiative in a two-boat race rests with the trailing yacht. The pressure is on her on the windward leg to try to break through the cover applied by the leader. On the leeward legs she must go wind hunting, try tacking downwind, or attempt to lure the top boat into a luffing match—anything that conceivably might help her situation. The leader's job is to parry each thrust, to counterpunch, to be alert defensively.

The tactics of the boat which is being beaten are determined to some extent by the relative speeds of the boats on different points of sailing, suspected weaknesses in the crew of the leader, demonstrated strengths in the trailer, by the desperateness of the situation, and the competitive urge of the loser's skipper.

Going to windward, a boat which is quick in stays and accelerates rapidly under certain conditions could profit from a short tacking duel against a rival a little slower in these respects. Note the "certain conditions" qualification. The reasons for it were sharply revealed in the *Gretel-Weatherly* tussles. In the rough, windy second race, *Gretel* came about and filled away faster than *Weatherly* and consequently gained so much that *Weatherly* broke off the fight while she was still ahead. In the races sailed in light and moderate weather, *Weatherly*'s fore-reaching technique in tacking easily kept *Gretel* under control.

An underlying reason for short tacking is the possibility that through tension or fatigue the crew of the leading boat can be forced into an error of commission or omission which will result in a foul up, reduce the yacht's speed and thus allow the trailer to drive through into clear wind. Of course, there is always the possibility that the mistake might occur on the trailing boat. In that case she drops farther astern and her crew consoles itself with the knowledge that they at least tried. Certainly nothing is to be gained by docilely tagging along after the leading boat, hoping that her mast will fall over the side, or her keel drop off.

A boat which is superior to her rival on one point of sailing, but either equal or inferior on others has the task of staying close enough to the enemy in his conditions so as to be able fully to exploit her advantage on subsequent legs. Here is an example: a fast off-the-wind boat hanging onto a faster windward working yacht on the weather leg so that she does not have to make up too much distance going downhill.

There was something of this nature in 1934, when the first *Endeavour* came so close to wresting the Cup from *Rainbow*. The English boat appeared to be faster all around, but her greatest margin over the defender was in running. Until *Rainbow* borrowed *Yankee*'s spinnaker and spinnaker expert, *Endeavour* outran her consistently. Whether this was because of the challenger's ventilated spinnaker, or better hull lines, or both is a matter of opinion. The fact remains that greater speed downwind gave the Britisher her first race triumph and the enormous lead she had in the third, until she threw it away on the last leg by making a completely unnecessary tack when she could lay the finish.

Vanderbilt described this race and its shifting fortunes as "a constantly changing panorama of breaks and mistakes." *Rainbow* made herself the beneficiary of the breaks, *Endeavour* made the mistakes.

This was to have been a leeward-windward race and started as such in a light breeze from northeast by east. When the wind hauled to the east, spinnakers were taken in, and balloon jibs set. Run or reach it made no difference to *Endeavour*. She turned for home 6 minutes 39 seconds ahead of the defender and seemed certain of her third consecutive victory.

She did not get it and why she did not has furnished fuel for many a yacht club fireside discussion since. It is one of the more bizarre incidents in the annals of Cup racing tactics.

When *Endeavour* rounded the lee mark, she could lie within two points of the finish on the starboard tack. By the time *Rainbow* came onto the wind, it had shifted to east-southeast and she could lay the committee boat.

The boats sailed in different breezes for a while: the English yacht in the weak, not so favorably angled breeze she had carried from the lee mark; *Rainbow* in a fresher, lifting slant. *Endeavour* was slightly on *Rainbow*'s lee bow, but a long way ahead. Only *Endeavour*'s sinking, it seemed, or the descent of an utterly flat calm, could change the picture. Vanderbilt turned the wheel over to Sherman Hoyt, who often steered *Rainbow* in light going, and went below to eat lunch and consider what measures he possibly could take to avoid becoming the first skipper to lose the Cup.

Even though *Rainbow* was pointing higher as she felt the new breeze, *Endeavour*'s legion of supporters felt no concern. All their boat had to do was hold her course until the approaching southeasterly slant reached her. When it did so, the challenger could come up to the course to the finish, and show *Rainbow* the way home as she had done in the previous two races.

T. O. M. Sopwith, *Endeavour*'s skipper, did not wait for the new breeze to reach him. He put the challenger about and sailed toward *Rainbow* and away from the finish, crossed the defender's bow with little to spare, and then tacked up to windward of her. Before *Endeavour* could gain full headway in the soft air, Hoyt sailed *Rainbow* through her lee, assumed the safe leeward position, and then squeezed up until *Endeavour* was backwinded and had to make two more painfully slow tacks to clear her wind. Those sealed her doom. *Endeavour* lost by 3 minutes 26 seconds.

Sopwith had been outsmarted by the wily Hoyt. *Endeavour* never should have tacked in the first place; didn't need to tack because, whether her navigator knew it or not, she was laying the finish. Sopwith had been deceived. The best person to tell how the diversion was accomplished is the little old warrior who planned and executed it. Hoyt chuckled over the incident in his memoirs in these words:

Because we . . . were aware of his [Sopwith's] tendency always to try and keep his opponent covered, I abandoned all attempts to sail the normal course home, which we could easily lay. I pointed as high as possible and foxed him into making his fatal tack toward us, but actually away from the finish line. From being well ahead on our lee bow, he barely crossed us, and . . . it was comparatively easy to pinch *Rainbow* a bit up under his lee bow, backwind him, force him to go about to clear his wind, then ease sheets and resume the course for the finish line of which our navigator [Professor Zena Bliss] had kept me constantly informed. The net result was that *Endeavour*, during the last leg home, had to come about four times while *Rainbow* fetched without a tack, having beaten *Endeavour* by 10 minutes on that leg.

There you have a classic example of a lost cause being saved because a tactician knew his opponent, was aware of a basic weakness in the other's doctrine, and applied psychological pressure to exploit it at the critical moment. *Rainbow* could not sail faster than *Endeavour*, but her afterguard could think quicker and sharper than their opposite numbers in the challenger's cockpit.

A boat trailing downwind can try to blanket the leader if she is close enough, and then sail around her to windward before she can recover. If the second boat is definitely the faster and the leg is long enough, her best course is through the leader's lee. If the first boat has a very large lead starting the leeward leg, then the trailer's best hope lies in tacking downwind, especially in light air. There is nothing to be gained by such a tactic when the boats are traveling at or near hull speed in a strong breeze right down the course.

Jock Sturrock, *Gretel*'s skipper, was the kind of a racing helmsman who never quit, never accepted defeat until *Weatherly* was across the finish line ahead of him. His strategy was to attack persistently on the wind or off it in an effort to take the lead from *Weatherly*. He was always trying to shake off Mosbacher's shackles. When *Weatherly* got the weather gauge on a windward leg, he short tacked until the spectators suffered vicarious exhaustion. The spine-tingling fourth race was definitely the closest and perhaps the most exciting in Cup history. Sturrock made it so on the last leg by his repeated efforts to blanket *Weatherly* with his fine American spinnaker as both boats stormed down to the finish in a freshening breeze.

Time and again *Gretel* luffed above *Weatherly*'s wake, trying to get on her wind. Mosbacher met each thrust with a precisely timed parry, hardening *Weatherly* up at just the right instant to avoid the blanket, falling back to the course when Sturrock retreated to gather himself for another attack. The fact that Sturrock did not get around Mosbacher is history. And as history it should be recorded that against only a slightly less gifted skipper than the man at *Weatherly*'s wheel, and a less accomplished, determined crew than that of the defender, Sturrock could have won.

It was also obvious to the more knowing observers that even though *Gretel* was bringing up a better breeze from astern, she probably would not have been in a position to exert such extreme pressure on *Weatherly* had she not been flying a beautifully shaped, Ted Hood-made spinnaker of extraordinary efficiency.

The place of sails in tactics is easily overlooked by those who never have been faced with the problem of deciding which weight and size of jib to use at the start of a race, which spinnaker to fly, which sails to carry as spares, and when and if to change headsails.

A Cup defense candidate which does not have a large inventory of first-class dacron and nylon dry goods in its sail bins is at a tremendous disadvantage in the selection trials. For proof, one need go no farther back than the observation trials of 1962, when *Easterner* was going through her locker day by day to determine through tests in actual competition which sails were worth keeping and which should be recut or rejected. All of her opponents were better off than she in the sail department at that stage of the season, and all of them at least matched her later improvements.

No less an authority on yacht racing than Cornelius Shields, Sr., a helmsman who has spent much of his lifetime achieving conspicuous success in major sailing competition, estimates that 75 per cent of any racing boat's prosperity can be traced to its sail equipment.

"No skipper can win consistently with poor sails," he has said times without number. "There is no ability, no mystico-magical touch nor anything else that will overcome this most serious disadvantage."

Hence the continuing quest for perfection in sails during a Cup campaign, the care and thought which the skipper gives every morning to the selection of which mainsail to bend on, what jibs and spinnakers to carry on board, which to have the tender take along for transfer to the racing yacht if the need for them arises just before the start of a match, and the meticulous records which some boats keep of sail performance.

When he was *Weatherly*'s skipper (1958–1961), Arthur Knapp kept a detailed log of which sails were used, in what conditions of wind and sea, when they were changed and why, and how efficient or inefficient they were in the circumstances. Knapp's sail record was an invaluable reference work for the crew that took over *Weatherly* in 1962, and the inspiration for a similar running evaluation written by her America's Cup navigator, Dick Matthews.

The start of Gretel's victory surge. In a smother of lifting white water, the big wave takes over Gretel's destiny.

Gretel (white spinnaker) roars up on Weatherly's weather quarter in a welter of foam and spray, leaving what looks like a steamer's wake. Weatherly (dark spinnaker), without benefit of assisting wave, is running at close to hull speed—not fast enough in this situation.

The most dramatic action of the 1962 Cup match occurred early on the final leg of the second race when Gretel rode the crest of a surging Atlantic roller past the defender and then sailed on to easy victory after Weatherly's spinnaker pole, sprung adrift by a parted afterguy, shattered itself on the jibstay.

Gretel, *a runaway on the crest of her private wave, is poking her nose past* Weatherly's *stern.*

Gretel *is abeam of* Weatherly *and about to rush by. All you can see of the Australian yacht is her skipper and the leech of her mainsail.*

Still flying like a surfboard on a wave-top, Gretel speeds into the lead.

After Gretel's wave has left her and she is reduced to normal speed under the brisk conditions, Mosbacher sharpens Weatherly's course to cross the challenger's stern and get into attacking position.

In the heavy breeze, the strain is too much for the after-guy's steel sinews. They snap; the aluminum pole, suddenly released, crashes against the jibstay and breaks like a stick.

"Well, what do you know about that?" Weatherly's fore-deck men seem to be saying as they look at the wreck of the spinnaker pole.

Weatherly *has her desired position out to weather of* Gretel, *but it is of no use to her now. She is going to lose speed and distance while her crew is clearing away the wreckage, rigging a new guy and spinnaker pole.*

Weatherly *isn't sinking—just a large wave between her and the photographer's boat as both dropped into troughs simultaneously—but her hopes are.* Gretel *has gone.*

In the course of her successful campaign for the defense assignment in 1962, *Weatherly* used to leave her berth with five jibs, two or three No. 1's of various weights of cloth, one No. 2, and one No. 3 for heavier going; three or four spinnakers, one a ¾ ounce drifter, the others 1¼ or 1½ ounce and cut either for running off or reaching, and a hankless, or so-called interim, jib, to set while shifting from one hanked headsail to another.

Weatherly had eight mainsails in her locker, but used only three of them her winning summer. One was used only on practice spins, to save wear and tear on the two which were regarded as her best racing sails. Choice between them hinged entirely on what Bus and his confreres thought the wind was going to do—build up to significant weight and strength from a gentle beginning, hold its morning velocity, or moderate as the day progressed. The wrong estimate of the situation, that is, bending on the wrong mainsail for the conditions which eventuated, could very well result in defeat, especially if the opposing skipper made the right guess. Unlike jibs, mainsails cannot be changed in a closed-course race without conceding defeat. The process of taking one off the spars and bending another on, assuming one is available, takes too long.

Thus, every morning before *Weatherly* took *Skipper*'s towline, her navigator obtained the latest weather forecast. He and the captain studied the report, related it to the existing conditions, and then Mosbacher made his decisions:

which mainsail to use, whether to carry more light than heavy jibs, or vice versa. There was one constant: *Weatherly* never carried her high-cut reaching genoa on board on days when windward and leeward races were scheduled. That sail went into her bins only when the program called for triangular contests on whose reaching legs the reacher might be useful.

The final decision as to which jib to hank on the stay was made at the last practicable moment, to minimize the possibility of having to make a hasty, last-minute change and more work for the crew. Often it was as late as the preparatory signal when *Weatherly*'s choice was made. By and large the other Twelves did the same thing on days when conditions were uncertain.

After the start, a skipper may find that he is using the wrong jib for the conditions prevailing on the course. He then is faced with another decision: shift headsails now, or lug the one in use for the rest of the round, and make the change before the next windward leg. Will he gain more by an immediate change than he will lose while making the switch?

In such situations the hankless jib comes into play. It can be set on the spare halyard, the unsatisfactory jib taken in, and the replacement hanked on and set with a minimum loss of speed through the water, because the interim jib is working while the change is in process. Interim jibs are not as efficient as genoas fashioned expressly for the conditions which indicate the change. But to racing sailors there can be no doubting their value as a means of keeping the boat moving at somewhere near her best speed in the interim between dousing one sail and getting its successor set and drawing.

A boat laid out below like *Columbia* has a distinct advantage in headsail-changing situations. She has a loading chute below deck in which the substitute jib can be laid out ready for hoisting through a hatch well forward. A man standing on a small platform in this hatch, attaches the halyard to the head of the jib, and then clips the hanks on the jibstay as shipmates sweat the halyard aloft. This ingenious arrangement is far more efficient than man-handling the jib out of the bin, getting it up to the foredeck and doing all of the work out in the open where wind and sea make it difficult at times.

Weatherly, a great deal finer in her forward sections than *Columbia*, and not equipped with the 1958 defender's efficient devices for expediting headsail changes, often carried the wrong jib long after it had become relatively ineffective rather than slow the boat even more by putting a man out on her narrow bow to make the switch.

Mosbacher figured that the process of going from one hanked headsail to another by way of an interim jib took four minutes. That much time with *Weatherly* rooting into the seas because of a man's weight up in the bow sometimes did more damage to boat speed than it was worth in the long run. Yachts with fuller bow sections, of course, did not have this trouble.

Some of the disadvantages of holding onto the wrong jib instead of going to another were minimized by a Ted Hood innovation, the adjustable luff jib. The inventive Marblehead sailmaker, yacht designer, and skipper built headsails without luff wire, substituting tapes sewn in such a manner that the draft in the jib could be controlled by changing halyard tension.

The revolutionary zipper luff jibs, such as the one made in Ike Manchester's Padanaram sail loft for the Australians and used on 12-Meters for the first time by *Gretel* in her fourth race with *Weatherly*, make headsail changes almost a matter of seconds instead of minutes. It took *Weatherly's* crew a while to recover from the amazement with which they reacted to *Gretel's* first sail change that afternoon.

The Australian yacht had started in light going with *Vim's* old 3½-ounce hankless jib set in her foretriangle. When the wind freshened halfway up the weather leg, *Weatherly's* crew looked on in disbelief while what looked like a big white snake crawled rapidly up *Gretel's* jibstay. It was the new zipper luff jib, whose leading edge, devoid of hanks, folded around the stay and zipped up on itself as it was hoisted. In a trice the new sail was up, set, and drawing, the hankless jib dropped on deck and thrown below.

It was all done so quickly than many spectators close to the yachts missed the operation completely. Usually when a headsail change is made going to windward, a boat can count on losing about a length to her opponent. If *Gretel* lost anything with her prestidigitator's switch, it was only a matter of a few feet.

Whether the zipper jibs are, as claimed, superior aerodynamically because of their smooth entering edge, there is no question about their being enormously faster to set and douse. They go up as fast as the halyard can be hoisted after the bow man engages the zipper slide. All he has to do is sit there and hold the slide while the sail goes up the stay. The sail can be brought down in a heap with one tug on the zipper slide at a predetermined release point in the zipper teeth.

On 12-Meter yachts, which carry so many spinnakers, it is not unusual to have differences of opinion about which to set. Kites destined for reaching with the pole well forward are cut flat, some of them so much so that they can be carried effectively when the apparent wind is abeam. Fuller, rounder, high-shouldered sails are used when running square off or nearly so. Area is not as important as shape. In certain velocities and angles, a smaller jib can be much more effective than a huge bag. Many is the time a small kite has been kept full and drawing in light air when a larger spinnaker on an opposing boat has drooped in discouragement.

Vim lost one crucial race to *Columbia* in 1958 because, quite by mistake, she set the wrong spinnaker. The rivals, close as always, rounded the first weather mark overlapped. *Vim* sent up her small red-topped spinnaker and used it so effectively that she led *Columbia* around the lee mark. *Vim* held her lead upwind, but, on rounding for the run to the finish, set her large running kite instead of the small one which had done such a good job on the first leeward leg. She had not intended to do so; someone must have passed the wrong turtle up to the foredeck, and, in the flurry of activity incident to rounding the mark and getting squared away for the run, the error was not noticed until it was too late. The sail was up there and drawing.

Columbia set a small spinnaker and got home 12 seconds before *Vim*. Mosbacher, recalling the incident ruefully, said: "If we had had our small spinnaker up we could have luffed with *Columbia* at least. With the big bag up there we could not sail as high as she and so we couldn't luff to try to keep *Columbia* from passing us to windward."

Mistakes which lose yacht races are not always the sins of tacticians.

TO THE LADIES

Their Role in Cup Competition

It has been vouchsafed to few women to share actively with their men the excitement, competitive stresses, discomforts, rewards, and disappointments of America's Cup racing. In all the history of this international sailing spectacle, the names of only seven women have been recorded as members of a challenger's or defender's crew.

For their less fortunate sisters, Cup time has been a time of waiting in the fashion of mariners' womenfolk ever since men first went to sea.

The duties of the ladies of the afterguard varied with the times in which they lived and sailed. In the nineteenth century, when yacht racing definitely was a man's game, played roughly by professionals, they probably involved nothing more serious and strenuous than lending a spot of glamour, the softening influence of a feminine presence to the quarterdeck, perhaps a whiff of exotic scent to temper the tang of Sandy Hook's ocean breezes.

The last three women, at least, to sail in Cup matches made more practical contributions to the operation of the vessels in which they were embarked. Mrs. William P. Burton (*Shamrock IV*), Mrs. Thomas O. M. Sopwith (the *Endeavours*), and Mrs. Harold M. Vanderbilt (*Ranger*), kept time at the start for their helmsmen husbands, and then put their eyes and ears into their service for the rest of the race, keeping constant watch on the opposition, reporting gains and losses of relative distance, insuring that there would be no tactical surprise.

Having sailed usefully with their husbands in many a regatta, they were valued racing as well as conjugal partners. The occasional dependence of skipper upon his lady was pointed up sharply when Bill Burton, the first amateur British helmsman in Cup annals, was asked to sail *Shamrock IV* for Sir Thomas Lipton. Burton made it a condition of acceptance that Mrs. Burton be included in the afterguard as his timer. *Shamrock's* crew did not share their skipper's enthusiasm for having a female on board. It was obvious to Sherman Hoyt, the American observer on the Lipton yacht in its match with *Resolute* in 1920, that the paid hands resented Mrs. Burton's presence. The gallant Hoyt, however, "found her a pleasant shipmate, never the least in the way, and most unobtrusive."

The first woman to sail in a Cup race did so at a time when the proper milieu for a Victorian lady was her drawing room, not a racing yacht with all those men. Mrs. William Henn, wife of the retired Royal Navy officer who brought *Galatea* to the United States in 1886 to race *Mayflower*, managed quite properly to meet the social arbiters' standards and still be at sea. Her drawing room was the main cabin of *Galatea*, and, if there was any essential difference between it and the overstuffed salon of an English town house of that era, it was not evident to guests in what had become the Henn's permanent home.

The below-decks accommodations and appointments would send shudders through the bones of men accustomed to the bleak, skinned-out interiors of modern 12-Meter yachts. The Henns lived aboard their 102-foot cutter in all the plush comfort of their day; heavy draperies over the ports, portieres in doorways, leopard skins spread over oriental rugs on the cabin sole, ornaments on bulkheads and catchalls, a fireplace, and a dining table. They had Mrs. Henn's pets aboard, too—a monkey, a cat, and several dogs.

Having made the thirty-one-day passage from England to Marblehead in *Galatea*, it seemed perfectly natural for Mrs. Henn to remain aboard when the Cup match began. After all, it was her home, and neither she nor her husband saw any point in her going ashore merely because *Galatea* was going racing instead of cruising. What Mrs. Henn did besides take care of the pets, which were barred from going topside during the race, history does not record.

On the last day of the series, it is likely that her duties included nursing her husband, who became ill before the race and remained below for the duration of the contest. Because of his illness, Henn asked the New York Yacht Club race committee to shorten the course from the specified forty miles to thirty so that he could get to a doctor sooner. The committee, its judgment untempered by compassion, refused on the grounds that it did not have the power to change the conditions of the match. Henn turned command of *Galatea* over to his helmsman and designer, J. Beavor Webb, went below, and rested there while his yacht took her second defeat from the swift Yankee sloop.

Mrs. Henn started something. You could not call it a trend, or a vogue—it has been too sporadic—but at least it was the lowering of a barrier. Seven years later, when Windham Thomas Wyndham-Quin, fourth Earl of Dunraven and Mount-Earl of Dunraven Castle, Brigend, Glamorgan, Wales, and of Adare Manor, Adare County, Limerick, Ireland, came over to sail *Valkyrie II* against *Vigilant*, he signed on not one female, but two. They were his daughters, Lady Rachel Wyndham-Quin and Lady Eileen Wyndham-Quin. Their names are inscribed in the New York Yacht Club records as members of *Valkyrie*'s afterguard.

In those days, the reporting of international yachting was carried on for the most part by men well schooled in their trade and given strongly to emphasis on the technical and tactical aspects of America's Cup sailing. There was no time, or space, for frivolous comment on matters which had nothing to do with the operation of the contending vessels. One chronicler of the times, however, departed from the pattern, and we are indebted to A. J. Kenealy of *Outing* magazine for proof of the fact that at least one

⚓

This practical if not pretty vessel is King Tut, *a canal tug which served* Nefertiti *as tender and, while she was racing, doubled as an observation platform for* Nefertiti's *Coach Fred Lawton, spare hands, and guests.*

136

of the Wyndham-Quin girls sailed at least one race in *Valkyrie II.*

Mr. Kenealy wrote in his account of the match between *Valkyrie II* and *Vigilant:*

On the deck of *Valkyrie* was a charming feminine figure in blue serge cut in such a fascinating costume that it made all old bachelors want to swear off. It was Lady Rachel Wyndham-Quin, one of Lord Dunraven's daughters. But the fair lady was fated to bring no good fortune to her father's yacht. Commodore Gerry has often told me that his control of wind and weather does not extend farther east than Pollock Rip, and I think that Lady Rachel's influence on the elements does not reach to the westward of the Lizard.

When their contentious and controversial parent returned in 1895 with *Valkyrie III*, the girls came too, and in their official capacity as afterguard members. That was the year when Lord Dunraven outspokenly found fault with virtually everything connected with the conduct of his match with *Defender.* Subsequently, he made such reckless and easily disproved charges of ballast manipulation against his adversary that the New York Yacht Club kicked him off its roster of honorary members.

The *Defender-Valkyrie III* match was notable for something besides Lord Dunravern's wretched sportsmanship and the repeat appearance of his daughters. It saw a woman in the crew of a defending yacht for the first time. She was Mrs. C. Oliver Iselin, wife of the managing director of the syndicate which built and campaigned the American defender.

Mrs. Iselin was not only our first lady member of a Cup boat organization; she was also our second. When her husband assumed with *Columbia* the same office he had held in the *Defender* syndicate, Mrs. Iselin's name again appeared on the defender's roster. It also appeared with great frequency in the society journals and sports pages. She was, from all accounts, a lady of beauty and charm, with a flair for spectacular costumes not exactly in keeping with her New England upbringing.

Men and Women of the Outdoor World, a magazine of the nineties that devoted its pages to pleasant profiles of persons prominent in sports, ran a flowery feature on C. Oliver Iselin and his contributions to yacht racing. In it was this paragraph:

"His second wife . . . is an enthusiastic yachtswoman and her counsel and presence during a race are potent factors in his achievements. She is a charming woman of the demure, puritanical type, affects white gowns and natty sailor suits and is as hospitable and popular as she is attractive."

When the *Columbia-Shamrock I* contest dragged through seventeen October days in 1899 before three races were completed, the fact of a woman sailing in a Cup yacht was enough of a novelty to attract newspaper editors whose staffs had run out of things to write about Sir Thomas

Mrs. Harold S. Vanderbilt—Gertie to shipmates—was a working member of Ranger's afterguard and the last American woman to sail in an America's Cup match.

Lipton. The *New York Journal* made Mrs. Iselin the subject of a feature article and elaborate five-column picture layout.

"Mrs. Iselin, the Mascot of Columbia," the caption read over the pictures showing Mrs. Iselin with her husband on the defender's deck, and by herself in a portrait studio. "The only woman who ever raced on an American Cup defender."

The *Journal's* reporter wrote: "She has sailed on *Columbia* during all of her races or attempted races. She sailed on the *Defender* when she whipped the *Valkyrie* three years ago. She is extremely pretty and has charming, graceful and kindly manners."

Her on-board duties were described as "sitting quietly in the companionway where she is out of everybody's way. She is dressed handsomely but appropriately and encourages the sailormen by a pleasant word or smile as they go about their work."

It was noted that Mrs. Iselin had watched *Columbia's* construction, performed the christening rites for the new yacht at Herreshoff's in Bristol, sailed in all of her trials, and then, "inspired by her patriotism," had become a creator of sailing fashions.

Mrs. Iselin designed an effective and significant yachting costume of red, white and blue. The skirt was of white flannel and of the same length as a golf skirt. It was trimmed around the bottom with six rows of bright red silk braid. The coat was a dark blue Norfolk jacket with belt, collar and cuffs of red. She wore the jacket open, and the shirtwaist which it revealed was of fine French flannel laid in plaits which were piped in red.

She forsook this national costume for a more modified one last week. It was of cream white serge, trimmed with glistening gold braid. The skirt was plain and cut in the new clinging fashion. The waist was made with a tight-fitting back and a sailor blouse front. It was trimmed across the front with bands of gold braid, each band finished on the left side with a gilt naval button. Four straps of gold crossed each shoulder and each strap ended with a button. The sleeves had cuffs made of rows of gold braid and a broad band of gold formed the belt which fastened with a big solid gold buckle. The collar was high and straight and made entirely of gilt braid. Mrs. Iselin wore with this a necktie which is one of the new French novelties. It was of fine white linen tied in a knot with slashed ends. The knot was cloth of gold and the linen ends were finely hemstitched.

In this costume Mrs. Iselin was a striking picture as she sat in the companionway of the *Columbia*, doing what no other woman has ever done, watching an international race from the yacht of her choice.

⚓

Almost crowded off the end of the Newport Shipyard pier by exhilarated members of extemporaneous reception committee as Weatherly *approaches after her final victory in 1962 are, left to right, Mrs. Henry D. Mercer, Mrs. Don Matthews, and Mrs. Emil Mosbacher, Jr.*

More than three decades were to pass before the United States produced a successor to Mrs. Iselin. Mrs. Vanderbilt made her appearance on *Ranger* contemporaneously with Mrs. Sopwith's second tour of duty with her husband on *Endeavour II* in the last of the duels between the great Class J sloops.

Mrs. Vanderbilt had been a familiar sight on the defender all that summer, but her sailing costume was not one to challenge the brilliance of those Mrs. Iselin flashed on *Columbia*. On days when foul weather gear was not indicated, Mrs. Vanderbilt wore a simple, short-sleeved white cotton dress with buttons down the front, and a soft, white hat which kept the sun out of her eyes and the wind from blowing her hair about. Mrs. Sopwith turned out in a dark beret and white version of what Winston Churchill was to popularize a few years later as a "boiler suit," a one-piece coverall garment of great utility but no claim to chic.

Mrs. Sopwith and Mrs. Vanderbilt in a sense were working members of their husbands' crews. There was more to their jobs than sitting quietly in the companionway encouraging the hands with a pleasant word or smile. They dressed accordingly.

They were the last of the seven glamour girls of the yachting stage, ladies who played supporting but highlighted roles in otherwise all-male casts in America's Cup dramas. There might have been eight of these heroines had the

Hovey family's racing fortunes equaled its devotion to big-boat racing.

Sis Hovey, now Mrs. Sherman Morss, was with her father and brothers in their J boat campaigns in the late thirties. When the Twelves rescued Cup racing from moribundity twenty-one years after the tall ships had been laid up, eventually to succumb to the shipbreaker's hammer and cutting torch, the Hoveys—Sis included—were back in the fight for selection with *Easterner*. Sis, whose husband was *Easterner*'s navigator, was virtually a regular in the 1958 campaign, a working member of the cockpit gang. She sailed occasionally in the early part of 1962 and then retired to seagoing sidelines before the final trials.

This emphasizes a radical difference between Cup yachting today and what it was in its first eighty-five years. In the days when our ladies of the afterguard were included in Cup boat rosters, the actual sailing of the yacht, the back-breaking pulley-hauley, was in the leathery hands of professionals, anywhere from two to five dozen of them. Until 1920 the boats were even steered by professionals. All the amateur afterguard did, presumably, was to direct operations, lend an official air to proceedings, and keep the

⚓

Mrs. T.O.M. Sopwith sailed in the afterguards of two Cup challengers, Endeavour *and* Endeavour II. *She's shown here at the wheel of the first* Endeavour *with her husband.*

captain company. There was no reason why, under those circumstances, a woman could not go along as timer or decoration or both.

It is quite a different story in the Twelves. They are much smaller boats than were their predecessors—less than a fifth of *Ranger*'s tonnage—and their complement is only eleven persons, a figure which includes helmsman, navigator, afterguard, and everyone else. There is no billet, with the possible exception of steering and navigation, which even a richly experienced, highly skilled woman sailor can fill in a 12-Meter racing organization.

Everyone, the navigator included—he has to tail the mainsheet or set up a backstay now and then—has to have tough hands, strong muscles, emotional balance, and great physical stamina. Ladies, other than Russian shot putters, rarely fit that picture. And because there is no room on a Twelve for passengers, it is not likely that we shall see women in America's Cup crews so long as the 12-Meter Class remains the contesting medium.

They also serve their husbands' cause, nevertheless, who nibble their fingernails and twist handkerchiefs into moist knots while watching their men striving for the old silver pitcher. Separated from them by a few hundred yards of rolling swell, or white-capped chop, they suffer or rejoice as the tides of their men's fortunes ebb and flow, experiencing the tensions and tortures peculiar to a sailor's wife. And when the tired sailors step onto the pier at the end of a grueling day, the wives are there, waiting. There are smiles and congratulatory kisses for the winner, words of sympathy and encouragement for the loser. Ask any good skipper what this means to crew morale.

Behind every successful Cup crew there is at least one unpublicized heroine whose name appears in no yacht club records, who receives no encomiums, no mementos of the campaign at victory celebrations. Her share in the effort has had nothing to do with stop watches, speed gauge readings, and what is going on in the enemy camp.

Her concern is with such workaday activities as the compiling of guest lists, devising menus for sailors' shipboard luncheons and headquarters dinners, directing a household staff, being a gracious and thoughtful social hostess, and a family leader of monumental patience, tact, and staying power. She is the lady who presides over the shore establishment a Cup crew calls home when it moves to the scene of the elimination trials.

Lucie Bedford Cunningham did such an outstanding job for the *Columbia*s as mistress of Beech Bound Manor in 1958 that many of her charges are still lyrical about it. She did not even mind—very much, that is—when they hung spinnakers to dry in the lofty entrance hall of the big house. She had been born into a sailing family, married a yachtsman, raised sailing children, and thus more or less expected this sort of thing, however disconcerting it might have been to her non-sailing guests.

Near the other end of Ocean Drive in Newport, where her husband had leased an estate so well equipped with houses that he was able to shelter in great comfort all of *Vim*'s young married couples and still have room for bachelor quarters, Dorothy Matthews mothered sailors and their wives as though they were her own children, as indeed some of them were.

Four years later, lovely Pat Mosbacher, who had been one of Mrs. Matthews' guests, became hostess of Seafair, the spacious establishment where the *Weatherly* crew lived in a fashion to which they readily became accustomed. By some alchemy of personality she contrived to run the place as a successful blend of exclusive resort hotel, college fraternity house, and the warm, friendly home of a very large, cohesive, lively, and interesting family—an achievement that contributed significantly to the high morale of the *Weatherly* team. A happy ship is an efficient ship.

Mrs. Mosbacher deprecated her own part in the proceedings. "Everything was so well set up for us at Seafair and we had such extremely nice, competent people on the staff that it was easy. The staff, many of them hotel trained, were used to doing things for a number of people and sometimes on short notice, so I had very little to do, really."

Nothing much, that is, except to collect and correlate the mimeographed guest invitation forms which the crew filled out at breakfast so that she knew how many guests to plan for at dinner that night, consult the housekeeper and chef about what to serve, prepare luncheon menus which would satisfy the ravenous appetites of *Weatherly*'s crew and those who rode in her tender, preside over social evenings organized or spontaneous, find places at the table for unexpected guests, see that everything about the house went well, that all hands were happy, that no frictions developed, and, at the same time, be an understanding wife to a husband burdened with a never-ending procession of problems.

Because Seafair was not a dry ship, Mrs. Mosbacher never had to play angel of mercy as did Mrs. Cunningham at Beech Bound. Alcohol was forbidden in *Columbia*'s camp, and its use outside was not exactly cheered by the high command, most of whom were teetotalers. Not so two members of the working crew. They were accustomed to treating tired muscles and nerves at the end of a hard day afloat with therapeutic doses of something stronger than milk and ginger ale. For these renegades and their wives, Lucie kept a first aid kit. Before dinner, she would meet them in a room away from other residents, produce from the recesses of her sewing bag the necessary ingredients, and then join her patients in thirst-quenching operations.

Nan Bainbridge, wife of *Weatherly*'s one-man engineering staff, took one responsibility into her hands. She drifted into the job of hostess on *Skipper*, the motorboat which daily carried *Weatherly*'s spare sails, crew standbys, technical observers, photographers, *Weatherly* wives, and guests.

Her husband's shipmates christened her "*Skipper*'s den mother."

They serve the Cup yacht's cause who do those chores which assume disproportionate importance only when they are not done well, unobtrusively, and without thought of reward. These ladies ran their part of the *Columbia*, *Vim*, and *Weatherly* operations that way.

Columbia and *Vim* in 1958, and *Weatherly* in 1962 were the outstanding boats of those campaigns, a circumstance which lends support to the theory that there exists a strong link between the kind of lives crews live ashore and the manner in which they perform afloat.

To the ladies, the unsung heroines of the battles of Newport!

THE DEEDS OF GIFT

A Study in Progressive Sportsmanship

In the days of the first challenges the deed of gift was looked upon largely as an instrument devised to keep the America's Cup in possession of the New York Yacht Club and was interpreted accordingly. Year by year in deference to strong outside pressures, concessions have been made, precedents have been established and the deed of gift has been remodeled until late races have been sailed under conditions very different, vastly fairer, and more in accordance with the increased dignity and importance of yacht racing than ever in the past.

The deed of gift has of late been interpreted more nearly in the spirit of its great donors as the most potent factor ever devised for the advancement and development of American yachting through the stimulus of international competition. . . . As more liberal terms have been made, the America's Cup has risen in value until from a mere relic it has become what its donors intended—the emblem of national supremacy in yachting.

So timely is this concise summary of progress from tenacious obstructionism to genuine sportsmanship in the administration of America's Cup affairs that it might have been written yesterday. But it was written three-quarters of a century ago by the late William P. Stephens, then yachting editor of *Forest and Stream*, who was to become American sailing's most respected historian.

What inspired that article and others by the same authority was the New York Yacht Club's decision after the *Volunteer-Thistle* match of 1887 to return the Cup to the last survivor of the original donors, George Lee Schuyler, with a request that he meet with a special committee and draw up a new deed of gift to replace that which he had written only five years earlier.

Mr. Schuyler, then seventy-six years of age, acquiesced. He met on several occasions with Commodore Elbridge T. Gerry and his five colleagues to work out the details of the document. What they produced was greeted with widespread disapproval on both sides of the Atlantic and so effectively smothered interest in Cup competition that not until the arrogant Lord Dunraven strode onto the scene six years later was the series resumed.

That racing for the Cup was able to survive not only Dunraven but the new deed of gift is eloquent proof of its resilience and durability.

The monument of legalistic circumlocution was signed on October 24, 1887, and is still in force today, although in somewhat altered form. One major revision and some clarifying resolutions have kept it up to date. Primarily, though, what has made it work has been the enlightened attitude of the men who have administered the New York Yacht Club's America's Cup policy in this century. Their willingness to waive the onerous provisions of the requirement for ten months' notice of challenge and full information on name, size, etc., of the challenging yacht, and their liberal use of the deed's mutual-agreement clause has been in keeping with what W. P. Stephens described as "the spirit of its [the Cup's] great donors."

The course of America's Cup history is easily traced by

studying the three deeds of gift which have governed the competition at different periods and the changes which time, public opinion, and a better understanding of what constitutes a fair match have wrought in the rules.

The original deed of gift was merely a letter which set forth in plain English the uncomplicated, straightforward, and eminently fair conditions under which America's Cup competition should be conducted.

The epistle was prepared by five of the six men—one had died in the interim—who formed the syndicate that built *America* and carried out her successful invasion of British waters. Its acceptance resulted in the transfer of the trophy from the drawing room of Commodore Stevens' home in Washington Square to the technical custody of the club, although it spent most of its time in Tiffany's vaults.

In view of the chauvinism which characterized the club's early administration and interpretation of the deed, and as a contrast to the smothering legal jargon of the present instrument, the letter is worthy of its prominent place in the history of yachting. Here it is:

NEW YORK
July 8, 1857

To the Secretary of the New York Yacht Club:

SIR:—The undersigned, members of the New York Yacht Club and late owners of the schooner yacht *America,* beg leave through you to present to the Club the Cup won by the *America* at the Regatta of the Royal Yacht Squadron at Cowes, England, August 22, 1851.

The Cup was offered as a prize to be sailed for by yachts of all nations without regard to difference of tonnage, going around the Isle of Wight, the usual course for the Annual Regatta of the Royal Yacht Squadron, and was won by the *America,* beating eight cutters and seven schooner yachts which started the race.

The Cup is offered to the New York Yacht Club, subject to the following conditions:

Any organized Yacht Club of any foreign country shall always be entitled, through any one or more of its members, to claim the right of sailing a match for this Cup with any yacht or other vessel of not less than thirty or more than three hundred tons, measured by the Custom House rule of the country to which the vessel belongs.

The parties desiring to sail for the Cup may make any match with the Yacht Club in possession of same that may be determined upon by mutual consent; but in case of disagreement as to terms, the match shall be sailed over the usual course for the Annual Regatta of the Yacht Club in possession of the Cup, and subject to its Rules and Sailing Regulations—the challenging party being bound to give six months' notice in writing, fixing the day they wish to start. This notice to embrace the length, Customs House measurement, rig and name of vessel.

It is to be distinctly understood that the Cup is to be the property of the Club, and not of the members thereof, or owners of vessels winning it in a match; and that the condition of keeping it open to be sailed for by Yacht Clubs of all foreign countries, upon the terms above laid down, shall forever attach to it, thus making it perpetually a Challenge Cup for friendly competition between foreign countries.

> J. C. STEVENS
> EDWIN A. STEVENS
> HAMILTON WILKES
> J. BEEKMAN FINLEY
> GEORGE L. SCHUYLER

The club's idea of mutual consent was having the match sailed wholly under its terms. It sent multiple defenders against the first two challengers and conducted most of the early races over what was known as the "inside course" in New York Harbor, where there was a heavy premium on local knowledge and great opportunity for interference with the contestants.

It was even necessary at one point before James Ashbury came over with his second challenger, *Livonia*, for Mr. Schuyler to explain to the New York Yacht Club what the Cup donors had meant by "match." What precipitated this was Mr. Ashbury's insistence that New York should meet his challenger with one vessel instead of a fleet as it had done the year before, and Commodore James Gordon Bennett's turning of the matter over to Mr. Schuyler for interpretation.

This is what he wrote in reply:

I think that any candid person will admit that when the owners of the *America* sat down to write their letter of gift to the New York Yacht Club, they could hardly be expected to dwell upon an elaborate definition of their interpretation of the word "match," as distinguished from a "sweepstakes" or regatta; nor would he think it very likely that any contestant for the cup, under conditions named by them, should be subjected to a trial such as they themselves had considered unfair and unsportsmanlike. . . .

It seems to me that the present ruling of the club (to sail a fleet against a challenging vessel) renders the America's trophy useless as a challenge cup. . . .

The club on March 24, 1871, accepted Mr. Schuyler's chiding, but only in part, adopting a resolution that "we sail *one or more* representative vessels, against the same number of foreign challenging vessels." When *Livonia* came to the starting line, New York had four vessels at its disposal to race against her—one at a time, the one to depend on the day's weather conditions. Actually, only two of the four were used, *Sappho* and *Columbia*.

Mr. Ashbury wrote a long letter to the New York Yacht Club afterwards complaining of "unfair and unsportsmanlike proceedings," and making it plain that if he ever came after the Cup again he would be accompanied by legal advisors because the New Yorkers "did not seem to be able to conduct races on the high moral plane" that existed in his country.

151

The arrival of the first Australian challenger for the America's Cup in this country.

In profile, Gretel shows her rectangular rudder, long, flat run aft, and powerful forward sections.

This stern view of the Royal Sydney Yacht Squadron hopeful gives an excellent idea of her hull form, particularly the flat-sided keel tapering to the rudder.

He succeeded at that moment only in angering the club to the point that the cups he had given to Commodore Bennett to be raced for by the New York fleet were returned to him with a curt note. By his unremitting protests against what he firmly believed to be a grossly unfair attitude toward challengers, he did, however, focus so much attention on the club's policy that the injustices he complained of eventually were moderated.

The first beneficiary of Ashbury's campaign for giving the challenger a sporting chance was the first Canadian contestant. Major Charles Gifford, vice commodore of the Royal Canadian Yacht Club, forced the multiple-defender issue when he was conducting negotiations in 1876 for a match for *Countess of Dufferin*. He asked point-blank whether New York would sail one boat against the Canadian, or "one out of four, as in Captain Ashbury's case, or whether it is to be an open race for all the yachts of the New York Yacht Club squadron."

New York gave a politician's answer: "A yacht will be at the starting point on the morning of each race to sail the match." A few days later it relented, agreed to name the defender before the match and to name only one. This history-making concession was the first crack in the armor of the club's arbitrariness.

After this and another woefully inept Canadian challenge were disposed of, the club came to the conclusion that the letter by which *America*'s owners had conveyed their trophy to New York was not sufficiently specific for the function which Commodore Stevens and his associates had expected it to perform. Whereupon, in December 1881, the Cup was returned to Mr. Schuyler, by then the only survivor of the donors. On February 2, 1882, he returned the prize with a new letter of gift and the club accepted both without delay.

Essential differences between the new instrument and the first were:

1. It made clear the obligation of the holding club to meet a challenger with only one yacht.
2. It specified that the challenging yacht must be constructed in the country she represented.
3. It required, in the interest of seaworthiness and good construction, that challengers must proceed to the site of the match on their own bottoms.

⚓

Shamrock III in drydock in Brooklyn before her match with Reliance. Almost like her conqueror, the British challenger reflected the extremes to which designers had gone toward the unwholesome skimming-dish hull form. After the Shamrock III–Reliance series, the New York Yacht Club adopted a rating rule which recognized displacement as well as sail area: by putting a premium on the former it encouraged the designing of more full-bodied hulls as opposed to flat-floored freaks.

4. A defeated yacht was barred from challenging again for two years or until another contest had intervened.
5. Eliminated Great Lakes clubs as challengers with these words: "Any organized Yacht Club of a foreign country . . . having for its annual regatta an ocean water course on the sea or on an arm of the sea shall always be entitled . . . to the right of sailing a match for this Cup."

The new document also stressed more strongly than did the first the national character of the trophy. This was accomplished by the provision that if a club holding the Cup was dissolved, the prize should be handed over to any eligible club of the same nationality as the club going out of business. Those who had maintained that the America's Cup belonged to the nation and that the New York Yacht Club was merely a custodian were delighted.

Three matches in three consecutive years were sailed under the new deed (1885 through 1887), and then suddenly the club decided that Mr. Schuyler should produce another with the assistance of a committee of five appointed for that purpose.

No one appreciated more than historian Stephens the problems confronting Mr. Schuyler and his confreres, and there were few yachting authorities in this country more keenly aware of the goal toward which they should be working. From his store of experience, he offered suggestions and two of his proposals found their way into the new document.

W. P., as Stephens later became affectionately known, had this to say of the project:

It is a most difficult matter for any body of men, however well informed, to frame conditions which shall be permanent and binding, and yet which will stand the test of time and of the constant change and improvements that are found everywhere. The vital importance of protecting such a trust as The Cup from any unauthorized tinkering, or even from too frequent changes good as well as bad, is too plainly evident to need proof; but at the same time yachting is constantly changing. Boats, methods and rules must improve with time and some provision must be made for the natural process of growth.

To meet these two conditions, then, but one plan is possible: the deed of gift must be framed broadly and must be based only on the general principles of fair play which govern all sports while as to minor details they must be left largely to interpretation of the general specifications in a liberal and sportsmanlike spirit, and to the establishment of such precedents as will insure adherence to these principles on the part of all to whom the temporary guardianship of The Cup may fall.

If the framers of the new deed read Mr. Stephens' article, they were unmoved by its appeal for fair play and the broad approach. They incurred the editorial wrath of writers on both sides of the Atlantic for a provision which required the challenger to reveal everything about herself ten months before the match, while the defender did not have to be named until "a time agreed upon for the start." The New York Yacht Club was attacked with enthusiasm on all fronts, and its protestations that it had to know all about the challenging vessel so that it would know what kind of a defender to build were rejected as poor excuses for poorer sportsmanship.

Even the mild-mannered W. P. Stephens let himself go. In an article carrying the headline, "AN ACT TO PREVENT YACHT RACING," he wrote:

If the object of the framers was to keep The Cup they had double reason to be proud for it not only promises to accomplish that end most effectively, but it does it in such a manner that in itself it is dear to the legal heart. Compared to the brief and simple phraseology of the former deeds, the new one is lengthy and verbose, it is put in the form of a legal agreement with covenants, parties of the first and second parts, successors and assigns, etc., etc., and like too many of its kind the full and elaborate provisions of its various clauses are robbed of their weight by the insertion of half a dozen words that might be passed by without notice on a casual reading, yet which outbalance all the rest of the document. Seemingly fair and liberal on its face, the deed is far more strict in its demands than either of the others, and the concessions made in favor of racing demands are all nullified in a single short clause.

He characterized the ten months' notice of challenge requirement as "preposterous," pointed out that six months always had been enough, and proclaimed that "the challenger must give all and get nothing in return."

Stephens was not the least bit mollified by the fact that the new instrument contained a one challenge at a time rule, as he had suggested, and also specified that all races should be sailed over ocean courses free from headlands and in waters deep enough for boats of 22-feet draft. He had scolded the club for holding in New York Harbor what he described as "a penny show in a puddle for the benefit mainly of steamboat owners," and argued that if the club "has any conception of the importance and dignity which international racing has now attained since Boston has taken it in hand [*Puritan, Mayflower,* and *Volunteer* were Boston-designed and owned] it will at once give up the inside course forever and further stipulate that all future races must be sailed on open sea courses . . . such as outside Sandy Hook, at Newport and at Marblehead." After the new deed was adopted, all Cup matches were sailed outside Sandy Hook until 1930, when the scene was shifted to Newport.

In this connection it is interesting to consider that the authors of the new deed were aware that New York had no monopoly on what Stephens called "mousetrap courses," and that if Britain won the Cup she could meet an American challenger on courses every bit as bad as those her representatives had been forced to sail in this country if there were no rule against it. Obviously, someone was thinking about The Solent's shoals and tides, and the Clyde's lofty headlands.

The vigor and universality of the condemnation heaped on New York after the publication of the 1887 document had some effect. Six months of dodging editorial brickbats convinced the club that some modification of the deed was indicated. In May 1888, when the Royal London Yacht Club asked for an interpretation of the deed, New York took refuge in the mutual-agreement provisions, and said that it considered as satisfactory the terms under which the races between *Genesta* and *Puritan*, *Galatea* and *Mayflower*, and *Thistle* and *Volunteer* were sailed, and therefore would accept a challenge under those terms.

It then nullified this gesture by adding as a condition of acceptance that, if the Cup were won by the challenger, it must be held "under and subject to the full terms of the new deed . . . the terms of which are distinct, fair and sportsmanlike."

Obviously, Royal London did not share this view. Nothing more was heard from this organization. A year later, the Royal Yacht Squadron challenged on behalf of Lord Dunraven's first *Valkyrie*, an 85-footer, and after three months of negotiation withdrew the challenge. It took the stand that acceptance of the condition at which Royal London had balked "would preclude the renewal of that friendly competition which it is so desirable to encourage and maintain, and for which the cup appears to have been originally conveyed to the New York Yacht Club."

The Squadron felt that agreeing to abide by the terms of the new deed would "compel it to insist upon receiving, should it be successful in winning the cup, more favorable terms from a challenger than those under which it challenged."

Nothing more was heard from the Squadron until it forwarded, in 1892, another challenge from Dunraven out of which came the *Valkyrie II-Vigilant* match of 1893. This challenge had been preceded by negotiations between Dunraven and a New York Yacht Club committee which produced an agreement that the load waterline length should be the only dimension required at the time of the challenge, and that if the Cup came into the custody of the Squadron it would be held "subject to challenge under precisely similar terms as those contained in this challenge."

Thus New York used the mutual-agreement clause of the deed to by-pass some of its disagreeable features, a precedent frequently followed thereafter.

The controversial deed of gift in its 1887 form read like this:

This Deed of Gift, made the twenty-fourth day of October, one thousand eight hundred and eighty seven, between George L. Schuyler as the sole surviving owner of the Cup won by the yacht *America* at Cowes, England, on the twenty-second day of August, one thousand eight hundred and fifty-one, of the first part, and THE NEW YORK YACHT CLUB, of the second part,
WITNESSETH—
That the said party of the first part, for and in consideration of the premises and of the performance of the condi-

tions and agreements hereinafter set forth by the party of the second part, has granted, bargained, sold, assigned, transferred, and set over, and by these presents does grant, bargain, sell, assign, transfer and set over, unto said party of the second part, its successors and assigns, the Cup won by the schooner yacht *America* at Cowes, England, upon the twenty-second day of August 1851. To have and to hold the same to the said party of the second part, its successors and assigns, IN TRUST, NEVERTHELESS, for the following uses and purposes:

This Cup is donated upon the conditions that it shall be preserved as a perpetual Challenge Cup for friendly competition between foreign countries.

Any organized Yacht Club of a foreign country, incorporated, patented, or licensed by the legislature, admiralty or other executive department, having for its annual regatta an ocean water course on the sea, or on an arm of the sea, or one which combines both, shall always be entitled to the right of sailing a match for this Cup, with a yacht or vessel propelled by sail only and constructed in the country to which the Challenging Club belongs, against any one yacht or vessel constructed in the country of the Club holding the Cup.

The competing yachts or vessels, if of one mast, shall not be less than sixty-five feet nor more than ninety feet on the load waterline; if of more than one mast they shall be not less than eighty feet nor more than one hundred and fifteen feet on the load waterline.

The Challenging Club shall give ten months' notice, in writing, naming the days for the proposed races; but no race shall be sailed in the days intervening between November 1st and May 1st. Accompanying the ten months' notice of challenge there must be sent the name of the owner and a certificate of the name, rig and following dimensions of the challenging vessel, namely, length of load waterline; beam at load waterline and extreme beam; and draught of water; which dimensions shall not be exceeded; and a custom-house registry of the vessel must also be sent as soon as possible. Vessels selected to compete for this Cup must proceed under sail on their own bottoms to the port where the contest is to take place. Center-board or sliding keel vessels shall always be allowed to compete in any race for this Cup, and no restrictions nor limitations whatever shall be placed upon the use of such center-board or sliding keel, nor shall the center-board or sliding keel be considered part of the vessel for any purposes of measurement.

The Club challenging for the Cup and the Club holding the same may, by mutual consent, make arrangement satisfactory to both as to the dates, courses, number of trials, rules and sailing regulations, and any and all other conditions of the match, in which case also the ten months' notice may be waived.

In case the parties cannot mutually agree upon the terms of a match, then three races shall be sailed, and the winner of two of such races shall be entitled to the Cup. All such races shall be on ocean courses, free from headlands, as follows: The first race, twenty nautical miles to windward and return; the second race an equilateral triangular race of thirty-nine nautical miles, the first side of which shall be a beat to windward; the third race (if necessary) twenty nautical miles to windward and return; and one week day shall intervene between the conclusion of one race and the starting of the next race. These ocean courses shall be practicable in all parts for vessels of twenty-two feet draught or water, and shall be selected by the Club holding the Cup; and these races shall be sailed subject to its rules and sailing regulations so far as the same do not conflict with the provisions of this deed of gift, but without any time allowances whatever. The challenged Club shall not be required to name its representative until at a time agreed upon for the start, but the vessel when named must compete in all the races, and each of such races must be completed within seven hours.

Should the Club holding the Cup be for any cause dissolved, the Cup shall be transferred to some Club of the same nationality, eligible to challenge under this deed of gift, in trust and subject to its provisions. In the event of the failure of such transfer within three months after such dissolution, said Cup shall revert to the preceding Club holding same, and under the terms of this deed of gift. It is distinctly understood that the Cup is to be the property of the Club subject to the provisions of this deed, and not the property of the owner or owners of any vessel winning a match.

No vessel which has been defeated in a match for this Cup can be again selected by any Club as its representative until after the expiration of two years from the time of such defeat, or until after a contest for it by some other vessel has intervened. And when a Challenge from a Club fulfilling all the conditions required by this instrument has been received, no other challenge can be considered until the pending event has been decided.

AND the said party of the second part hereby accepts the said Cup subject to such trust, terms and conditions and agrees to and with said party of the first part that it will faithfully and fully see that the foregoing conditions are fully observed and complied with by any contestant for the said Cup during the holding thereof by it; and that it

will assign, transfer, and deliver said Cup to the foreign Yacht Club whose representative yacht shall have won the same in accordance with the foregoing terms, provided said foreign club shall, by instrument in writing lawfully executed, enter with said party of the second part into the like covenants as are herein entered into by it, such instrument to contain a like provision for the successive assignees to enter into the same covenants with their respective assignors, and to be executed in duplicate, one to be retained by each Club, and a copy thereof to be forwarded to said party of the second part.

IN WITNESS WHEREOF, the said party of the first part has hereunto set his hand and seal, and the said party of the second part has caused its corporate seal to be affixed to these presents and the same to be signed by its Commodore and attested by its Secretary, the day and the year first above written.

GEORGE L. SCHUYLER (L.S.)
THE NEW YORK YACHT CLUB
by ELBRIDGE T. GERRY, *Commodore*
JOHN H. BIRD, *Secretary*

(Seal of the New York Yacht Club)
In the presence of H. D. HAMILTON

⚓

Moonlight and electric flood lamps lend a romantic touch to this unusual spectacle—three of the four American defense candidates hauled out on the Newport Shipyard ways for their last scrubbing, polishing, and drying-out the night before the final selection trials.

With occasional mutual consent variations on the basic theme, this document served through the two completed Dunraven challenges, Sir Thomas Lipton's five unsuccessful ventures and the two *Endeavour* contests without alteration. In 1956, nearly two decades after the last of the J boat matches, it became sharply evident that unless appropriate measures were taken to pump life into the moribund competition the Cup would disappear into the limbo reserved for sporting relics.

No longer was it financially feasible to build out-and-out racing yachts of 65 feet or more waterline length either in this country or Britain under the existing income tax scales.

It was at this low point in the Cup's career—never had so many years elapsed between challenges—that Henry Sears, then New York's commodore, decided to do something about the situation. He went to England and there discussed matters with yachtsmen interested in keeping Cup racing alive.

Obviously, one answer to the problem was to sail for the Cup in smaller boats. How small? In keeping with the importance of the trophy internationally, it had become the custom for challengers and defenders to be the largest racing craft in their respective countries. To drop too far down the size scale might diminish the old pitcher's stature as a symbol of international sailing supremacy.

At that time the largest pure racing boats active in either Britain or the United States were International 12-Meter Class sloops, all of prewar vintage. There were, however, on both sides of the ocean many large, modern ocean-racing vessels, some of them even larger (73 feet LOA) than the Twelves. Strong sentiment developed here and abroad to race for the Cup in these fine cruising boats; there was nothing in the deed to bar the type except the minimum waterline limit of 65 feet. None was that long. Neither, of course, was the 12-Meter.

It was argued by proponents of yachts built to the Cruising Club of America or Royal Ocean Racing Club specifications that anyone putting $200,000 or so into a boat would prefer something more for his investment than a racing

⚓

After two light weather races, there was a good breeze for the third race of the first America's Cup match sailed in 12-Meter yachts. "Sceptre weather," backers of the English challenger called it. They were wrong. Columbia (US 16) flogged the Britisher severely that day upwind and down. This photograph shows Columbia weathering Sceptre not long after the start. Note how Sceptre's mainsheet seems to lead to the center of the traveler while Columbia's is well down to the lee side where it should have been in a fresh breeze.

machine which would be virtually worthless if it were not fast enough to attain Cup status. Therefore, the cruising segment asserted, it would be easier to persuade people on both sides of the Atlantic to build candidates if cruising boats were approved. The unsuccessful candidates would still be good cruising boats, undoubtedly good enough to win a prize now and then in offshore or alongshore racing.

When the time came to make a decision, the cruising yacht supporters lost to those who felt that the largest pure racing yachts possible should carry on the tradition. When Sears received assurance from Royal Yacht Squadron friends that a challenge for a match in yachts built to the International 12-Meter Class rule of measurement would be forthcoming if the necessary changes could be made in the deed of gift, he returned to New York elated.

The club's trustees shared his enthusiasm and promptly approved the necessary legal steps. Because the last of the original donors had long since departed this life—Mr. Schuyler died a yachtsman's death in 1890, on board Commodore Gerry's steam yacht *Electra*—court approval of any changes in the trust was required. On December 17, 1956, an order of amendment was issued by the Supreme Court of the state of New York eliminating the rule that challenging yachts must sail to the scene of the match on their own bottoms—a 12-Meter yacht is hardly the most desirable vehicle for a transatlantic voyage—and reducing the lower limit on waterline length from 65 to 44 feet, a

figure which the Twelves could make without difficulty.

Instead of the tempest of criticism which blew up around the 1887 revision, there was only praise for these changes. A challenge came promptly from the Royal Yacht Squadron; *Sceptre* was defeated by *Columbia*, the survivor of eliminations involving three newly built 12-Meter boats and prewar *Vim*, and the Cup was rescued from threatened oblivion.

On March 27, 1958, the year that competition was resumed, New York's trustees plugged a possible loophole in the deed by enlarging upon the definition of the word "constructed" so that it meant insofar as Cup challengers and defenders were concerned "designed and built."

The resolution, now appended to the deed, reads:

Now, THEREFORE, in view of the expressed intent of the donors of the America's Cup that it should be "perpetually a Challenge Cup for friendly competition between foreign countries" and the fact that in accordance with that intent and commencing with the first race for the Cup in 1870 down to the present time every challenger has been both designed and constructed in the country of the challenging Club and every defender has been both designed and constructed in the country of the defending Club so that every challenger and every defender has been in all respects truly representative of the countries of the challenging and defending clubs and the Cup has become by tradition the symbol of the yachting supremacy of the country of the Club winning the challenge match;

Establishing relative positions. Nefertiti *(No. 19)* on starboard tack, weathering Columbia *(No. 16)* in one of their
1962 trial races.

RESOLVED that the word "constructed" wherever it appears in the Deed of Gift of the America's Cup shall always be construed as "designed and built."

New York was most liberal in its application of this resolution when Australia became a challenger for the first time on April 14, 1960. The extrusions from which *Gretel*'s masts were made were fabricated in the United States, one of her booms was fashioned here, her most effective sails were American-made and, because no comparable facilities existed in Australia, Alan Payne, *Gretel*'s designer, was permitted full use of the towing tanks of the Davidson Laboratory at Stevens Institute of Technology in Hoboken, New Jersey.

In fact, there were many well-informed persons who felt we had come perilously close to losing the Cup for the first time because the New York Yacht Club had leaned over backwards in its interpretations of the deed to help Australia put on a good show.

It was quite amply demonstrated at Newport in 1962 that the Australians did not need quite as much help as they had received. *Gretel* was a very fast yacht, perhaps inherently faster than the four-year-old *Weatherly*; gave a fine account of herself; won one race, and might easily have won others but for the tactical genius of the man at the wheel of the defender.

Gretel will be the last challenger, however, on which New York will lavish the largesse which was in such sharp contrast to its nineteenth-century attitude toward invaders. The 1962 experience and subsequent inquiries from potential challengers in other countries about the availability of American equipment and facilities moved the club's trustees to clarification—and tightening—of its "designed and built" interpretation.

Two months after the *Weatherly-Gretel* match, the trustees on December 7, 1962, adopted a resolution which barred towing tanks and other "design facilities" in the defending country to the challenger, and made it plain that the word "built" included components of the vessel, fittings, and sails. In other words, so long as the U.S.A. held the Cup, no challenger could test models in the Stevens tank, or buy masts, booms, winches, bar rigging, and sails in this country. If these facilities and equipment were not available in the challenging country, it could request New York's permission to obtain them elsewhere—but not here.

The resolution in full:

WHEREAS, certain citizens or subjects of foreign countries, members of yacht clubs which qualify under the Deed of Gift of the America's Cup, and which yacht clubs are considering challenging for the America's Cup, have raised the question as to whether the obtaining of components (other than raw materials), fittings and sails or the use of design facilities such as a towing tank, outside the country of the challenging club would be construed as falling outside of the Board's Resolution of March 27, 1958, construing the word "constructed" in the Deed of Gift as "designed and built"; and

WHEREAS, by Resolution dated March 27, 1958, the Board construed the word "constructed" wherever it appears in the Deed of Gift of the America's Cup as meaning "designed and built"; it is

RESOLVED, that the word "designed" includes the use of a design facility such as a towing tank, and that the word "built" includes components, fittings and sails; and

WHEREAS, the Board recognizes that components, fittings and sails and the availability of design facilities such as towing tanks may not be obtainable in the country of the challenging club; it is

RESOLVED, that recognizing that such design facilities may not be available and components, fittings and sails may not be obtainable in the country of the challenging club, the New York Yacht Club, at the instance of a challenging club, will consider a request for permission to obtain certain of the aforesaid components, fittings and sails and to use the aforesaid design facilities in any country other than that of the defending club;

RESOLVED, that whenever the Deed of Gift of the America's Cup is printed, this Resolution with preamble adopted December 7, 1962, and the Resolution with preamble adopted by the Board of Trustees on March 27, 1958, interpreting the word "constructed" to mean "designed and built," be printed with the Deed of Gift.

W. MAHLON DICKERSON
Secretary.

What all this means is simply this: Hereafter foreign yachts must be foreign in all respects.

Comparison of Class J and 12-Meter Boats

By superimposing to scale a sail plan of *Columbia* on that of *Ranger*, the design department of Sparkman & Stephens, New York naval architects, has provided this unusual and accurate comparison of the great, skyscraping Class J sloops which raced in the Thirties and the International 12-Meter Class yachts which took over in 1958. S. & S. were co-designers with the late W. Starling Burgess on the *Ranger* project and solely responsible for the design of *Columbia*. Last and fastest of the 135-foot J's, *Ranger* defended the Cup against *Endeavour* II in 1937. *Columbia* began the 12-Meter era by turning back *Sceptre* 21 years later. Here is a comparison of the yachts' vital statistics:

	Ranger	*Columbia*
Length overall	135′2″	69′5″
Length waterline	87′	45′6″
Beam	20′10″	11′10″
Draft	15′	8′11″
Sail area	7546 sq. ft.	1817 sq. ft.
Tons displacement	166	28.4
Mast height	160′	82′

Despite her great size, *Ranger* was not the largest boat to race for the Cup—the 143-foot *Reliance* (1903) has that distinction—but the 12-Meters definitely are the smallest of the Cup yachts. *Mischief* (1881) was only 67′5″ on deck, but her waterline was 61 feet, about 15 feet longer than that of today's Cup boats.

The drawing of the lines of this 12-Meter Class yacht is the work of naval architect Alvin Mason. It is a fine example of the breed, and shows the functioning of the formula by which all boats built to the 12-Meter rule must be measured.

Whenever the 12-Meter Class is mentioned, this question naturally arises: "Is it called a 12-Meter because it is 12 meters in size?"

The answer is a contradiction: "No" because the boat isn't 12 meters in any dimension and "Yes" because the quotient of the measurement formula must be 12 meters or 39.37 feet.

Here is the basic formula by which the rating length (39.37 feet or 12 meters) is obtained:

$$R = \frac{L + 2d + SA - F}{2.37}$$

R = rating; in this case, 12 meters.
L = length of hull measured at a point approximately 7 inches above the load waterline, with corrections for girth.
D = skin girth minus chain girth. Skin girth is measured on the surface of the hull from sheer to keel about amidships. Chain girth, taken at the same place, is what a line would measure if stretched taut between sheer and keel.
SA = sail area; mainsail area plus that of fore triangle (area bounded by mast, jibstay, and deck).
F = freeboard.
2.37 = mathematical constant.

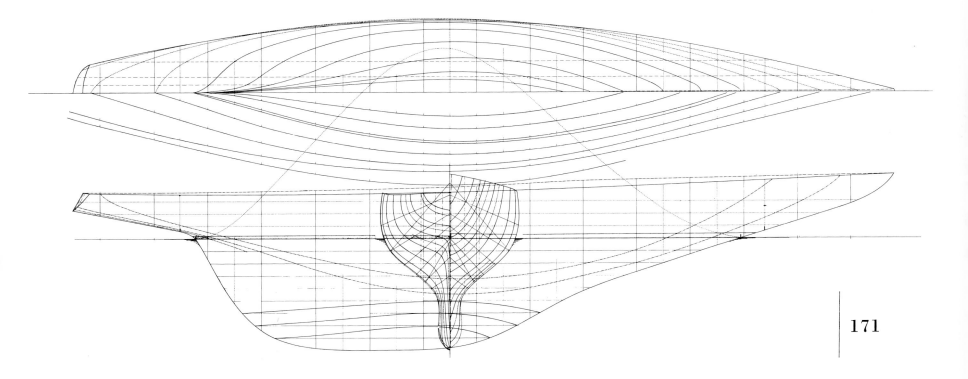

171

Mason's design for a boat 69 feet 7 inches overall, 46 feet 3 inches waterline, 11 feet 3 inches beam and 9 feet draft with 1854 square feet of sail area worked out to 39.37 feet in this manner: Corrected length (overall less overhangs plus girth adjustments) 53.92, plus skin girth minus chain girth .28, plus square root of sail area 43.06, minus freeboard factor 3.96, gives measurements of 93.30 which, divided by mathematical constant of 2.37, equals 39.37.

The purpose of the measurement rule to which about 100 boats have been built since its adoption by the International Yacht Racing Union in 1907, is to produce fast, long-lived, seaworthy racing yachts. Extremes are discouraged. This is accomplished by having the factors in the formula balance each other, imposing penalties for narrow beam and excess draft and encouraging high freeboard. The reverse sheer hull, esthetically offensive to many, is impossible under the rules so it is difficult to produce a really ugly boat.

If the length of the hull is increased, the amount of sail area has to be reduced otherwise the rating of 39.37 will be exceeded and the yacht will no longer be a 12-Meter.

Conversely, if the amount of sail on the spars is increased, either the length or girth factors will have to be reduced commensurately to obtain the same quotient. Sometimes changes are made within the desired sail area figure by increasing the size of main or jib and decreasing the other accordingly.

The rule limits mast height above deck to 82 feet and the height of the jibstay to 75 per cent of this dimension. In addition, the minimum weight (including all attached fittings), diameter, and center of gravity of masts are specified. Consequently it pays the designer to work as closely as possible to the limits. Jibs must be triangular in shape (the quadrilateral or "Greta Garbo" headsails of the J boat days are now illegal) and they cannot extend more than 15.7 feet aft of the mast. Spinnakers are limited in width to 2½ times the length of the spinnaker pole, whose length in turn is controlled by that of the foretriangle. In other words, the longer the foretriangle, the larger the spinnaker. *Nefertiti*, shown under spinnaker on the jacket of this book, had the largest foretriangle of any 12-Meter. Hence her enormous kite.

A LOOK AHEAD

The Line Forms to the Right

The 1956 revision of the deed of gift which made International 12-Meter yachts eligible for the America's Cup not only brought the competition back to the racing calendar after an absence of twenty-one years, it also widely broadened the field of possible challengers.

Whether this development was intentional or an unexpected by-product of the change is immaterial. What is important is the fact that the Twelves are authentically international and can be built and raced for a figure comprehensible even to those not associated with the U.S. Bureau of the Budget. The way is thus open for many other nations to move into a segment of sailing which virtually had been a United Kingdom–United States monopoly.

Australia broke the transatlantic chain of challengers in 1962, and has served notice that she will sail again at the first opportunity. The Scandinavian countries, with their great seafaring traditions and long association with the International Rule classes, must always be considered possibilities. Italy may be classed as a probability; a delegation of Italian yachtsmen watched the 1962 match at Newport and conferred with New York Y.C. officials about a challenge in the near future. Just how near is in the realm of pure speculation, New York having made it abundantly plain that if its defender defeats the Royal Thames challenger in 1964, at least three years will elapse before the next match.

This was stated in a policy bulletin issued by the club on December 7, 1962, under the title "New York Yacht Club Memorandum Regarding Future Challenges for the America's Cup." The necessity for such a memorandum undoubtedly stemmed from two sources: first, the club's realization that because active interest in Cup racing no longer was limited to the United States and Britain, several challenges might materialize at once; second, a desire to avoid repetition of the unfortunate and totally unnecessary dissension which accompanied the rejection of a Royal Thames challenge for 1963 and the acceptance of one for a year later.

The memorandum that resulted attempted to tie down some loose ends. It established guidelines for future negotiations in the following words:

I. *Assuming that the New York Yacht Club is successful in defending the British challenge in 1964.*

If the New York Yacht Club wins the Match with the Royal Thames Yacht Club in 1964, it will, while holder of the Cup, receive challenges made in accordance with the Deed of Gift, and will consider all challenges in the order of their receipt. If, however, two or more challenges are received within thirty (30) days of the termination of the Match to be sailed in 1964, or other subsequent matches, such challenges will be regarded as received simultaneously, and the New York Yacht Club, after due consideration, will determine which challenge to accept.

175

II. *There can be no substitution in the case of a defending club.*

While by mutual agreement between the challenging and defending clubs there may be a substitution of one challenging club for another of the same nation, there can be no substitution in the case of a defending club, and the defending yacht should be designed and constructed in the country of the defending club.

III. *If the New York Yacht Club loses a Match for the Cup it can have no control over the policies of the new defending club.*

Where the Cup is held by a club other than the New York Yacht Club, it is held solely subject to the provisions of the Deed of Gift and it may take any action which it deems best in connection with the acceptance of challenges provided such action is consistent with the terms of the Deed of Gift.

IV. *The Class in which contests for the Cup will be held.*

For the present, the New York Yacht Club, as the holder of the Cup, expects to defend it in the International 12-Meter Class, and it will give two years' notice of any intention on its part to change to another Class.

V. *Interval between Challenges.*

The New York Yacht Club believes that it is neither practical nor desirable that Matches for the America's Cup should be held each year, and it further believes that it would be in the best interests of the sport and of the competition for the America's Cup if such matches were not held more frequently than once in three years.

With this memorandum the club left few doubts as to how it would conduct Cup business so long as the trophy remained at 37 West 44th Street. For one thing, it forestalled the likelihood of the ludicrous spectacle of two or three foreign representatives simultaneously trying to thrust challenges into the hands of the New York commodore the instant the defender won the deciding race.

In the same section New York assumes full responsibility for the selection of the next challenge, if its defense prevails. It does not leave itself the refuge from criticism provided by a first-come, first-served clause. Thereby hangs a question: Who, assuming a U.S. victory in 1964, will succeed to the challenger's role?

It appears certain that no matter who wins in 1964, Australia will file her second challenge. *Gretel*, a fast boat, came very close to winning in 1962 and underwent changes in 1963 calculated to make her even faster. Any new Twelve Australia produces—and one has been promised—will have to prove herself superior to the Royal Sydney Yacht Squadron's pride before she goes overseas in quest of the Cup.

⚓

Who said spinnaker? Here's the largest and most colorful of all the American 12-Meter kites—Nefertiti's buxom red, white, and blue monster pulling efficiently with a low-cut, narrow spinnaker staysail set to catch whatever air, if any, is missed by that bulbous circus tent above it.

Italy must be regarded as a very likely challenger and, if history means anything, England is not going to drop from the America's Cup lists just because she loses another match.

This presents the possibility of New York having to choose among three challengers. Whatever the decision it is not going to please everyone, particularly those nations which then face the discouraging prospect of at least three more years of waiting.

The multiple challenge possibility, if not probability, suggests a solution which would have the virtue of giving everyone the desired opportunity and at the same stroke minimizing the likelihood of discouraging Cup competition interest in new countries. If, for instance, three challenges were received within the prescribed 30-day period, New York could arrange a series of elimination matches among yachts of the clubs concerned and accept the survivor as the challenger.

Such a method of winnowing out aspirants, not unlike the Davis Cup round structure in tennis, insures every challenger an opportunity to race and leaves the defender to meet the strongest. There is nothing in the deed of gift to outlaw this device.

It would stimulate competition in two ways: first, challenge-round racing would be keener because the challenger will have proved her right by something more meaningful than merely placing the necessary piece of paper in New York's hands before anyone else; second, interest would become more widespread—there would be no long line of prospective challengers forming with no guarantee that everyone in it ever would get to race for a trophy whose donors intended "as a perpetual challenge cup for friendly competition between foreign countries."

All that is required is the elimination of the phrase, "of the same nation" in Section II of the December 7, 1962, memorandum. The premise that if too many countries become involved the Cup will lose its lustre is hardly tenable. Certainly the Davis Cup has not diminished in importance because it is challenged for every year by a multitude of tennis-playing nations.

By the provision against substituting defenders, New York interprets the deed as prohibiting this practice and is forestalling any moves in that direction. Under the latest interpretation, for example, if Royal Thames should win the Cup and accept a challenge from an American club, it could not turn its defense responsibilities over to an Australian organization, or for that matter, to the Royal Yacht Squadron. It could, however, name a R.Y.S. yacht as its defender assuming that the owners would agree to race under Royal Thames auspices.

There is precedent for this in New York's own defense of the Cup. *Puritan*, which defeated *Genesta* in 1885, was built by a syndicate of Eastern Yacht Club members and enrolled in the fleet roster of the Marblehead citadel of sailing in the name of Edward Burgess, her designer. She flew his private signal in all of the trial races and in the match with *Genesta*. The question arose, naturally, as to whether *Puritan* had not won the Cup for Eastern since Burgess was the vessel's legally responsible owner of record and was a member of Eastern, not of New York.

The latter nimbly escaped from this trap by countering with the word that General Charles J. Paine, one of *Puritan*'s owners, was a New York member and the yacht had been entered in the trials and Cup races in his name. Interestingly enough, *Puritan*'s name did not appear in the club's 1885 year book. Someone thought quickly in this emergency.

The question never arose again because the next two Massachusetts challengers raced under General Paine's ownership and colors as New York Yacht Club vessels. In 1962, when *Nefertiti* was campaigned by a Boston syndicate, its two principals were admitted to New York membership before the trials began, just in case.

The words "of the same nation" in the clause permitting the transfer of a challenger's rights from one club to another, effectively preclude any such arrangement as New York was prepared to accept before the 1962 match.

When Australia's unexpected challenge early in 1960 took England by surprise, Royal Thames enlisted the aid of Prince Philip in an attempt to get the Royal Sydney Yacht Squadron to agree to British Commonwealth trials, the winner of which would then meet the American defender. New York, in the interest of insuring that the challenger would at least be an improvement on the woeful *Sceptre* of 1958, was willing to accept a possible substitute challenger, but nothing came of all this because the Australians, having beaten the mother country to the draw, were not about to yield their prerogative. They turned down the Prince's plea and Royal Thames had to settle for first chance after 1962.

There was a story going the rounds of yachting circles in 1963 that Sydney yachtsmen, eager for another try at the Cup at the earliest possible date, had sent out feelers to England after the acceptance of the Royal Thames challenge, suggesting the desirability of much the same arrangement which Prince Philip had put forward three years earlier. They were not surprised to find the English attitude very much like their own had been. This is all academic because, for Cup purposes at least, Australia is now considered a country in her own right, and the new rule prohibits any such transfer of challenging rights.

New York also states in its policy memorandum that if it loses the Cup it will have nothing to say about how the defending club handles negotiations with respect to subsequent challenges so long as they are in keeping with the deed of gift. Therefore anyone who takes the trophy away from its present home is under no obligation to feel bound by New York's decision that the Cup should not be

The serious business of competing for selection as an America's Cup defender sometimes has its lighter moments; light, that is, for the spectators, embarrassing for the contestants. More often than not there's a spinnaker behind the comedy relief. In one of her trials—she fortunately had an enormous lead at the time—Weatherly's spinnaker was washed out of its turtle by an errant wave. The top of it filled with air, the rest of it with water, and Weatherly was almost dragged down onto the turning mark. We see her sheepish crew hauling the soaking truant back on board. Nefertiti's outsize spinnaker was particularly susceptible to twists and the second photograph shows a snarled acre of nylon. The crew is lowering the jib in the hope of helping the situation. It didn't. Eventually the whole writhing, squirming mess had to be brought down on deck, thrown below, and another spinnaker sent up.

raced for more often than once in three years. It is New York's contention that more frequent contests, besides imposing severe strain on the financial and manpower resources of the clubs involved, would endanger the Cup's pre-eminence in the world of sailing.

New York had a difficult time after the *Weatherly-Gretel* contest convincing the British that it meant exactly what it said when its flag officers and Cup committee members conveyed to Royal Yacht Squadron and Royal Thames Yacht Club representatives at the match that it wanted a year's respite before embarking on another defense project.

It was purely and simply a matter of economics and personnel availability. Financing new boats, recommissioning others, finding people to man them and supervise their trials who could afford to give up an entire summer two years in a row, was out of the question. All of this was explained to the British officials at Newport while informing them that while a challenge for 1963 could not be entertained, one for 1964 would be welcomed.

It was therefore surprising when, less than a month later, the Royal Thames forwarded a formal challenge for a 1963 match. New York, understandably irked, abruptly rejected the challenge, an action which upset those Englishmen who apparently felt that if they put the question formally and publicly to the defender, New York might not have the courage to refuse.

They learned to their discomfiture that New York was not to be bluffed out of the stand it had taken during private September conversations among Major Charles Ball, vice commodore of the Royal Thames, Peter Vanneck, Royal Yacht Squadron representative, Commodore H. Irving Pratt, the chairman of the Cup committee, Henry S. Morgan, and other New York officials.

There was much moaning in some sections of the British press that the American refusal imposed great burdens on the British by refusing the challenge; that it would add substantially to their expenses and make it difficult to keep a crew together. The fact that they had been made well aware of the New York Yacht Club attitude well in advance was conveniently overlooked.

The British claim to the right to a match in 1963 was based on a letter written to Royal Thames in 1960 after the London club had been outmaneuvered by Australia in the presentation of a challenge for a match in 1962. This message, written on May 12, 1960, by W. Mahlon Dickerson, New York Yacht Club secretary, when the Royal Thames challenge arrived after Royal Sydney's had been accepted, stated: "*To the degree that it can be foreseen at the present time* and in the event the New York Yacht Club retains The Cup, the New York Yacht Club would be prepared to accept from a qualified club a challenge for 1963."

Ignoring the italicized qualifying phrase in Dickerson's

letter, the Earl Mountbatten of Burma, commodore of Royal Thames, followed the club's cabled challenge with a letter in which he said: "I feel sure you will not mind if we ask you to be so kind as to stick to the date you yourself proposed."

That so heavily qualified a statement could be construed as a firm commitment to accept a challenge suggests a great deal of wishful thinking in Knightsbridge. Royal Thames's official explanation of its insistence on 1963 was that prospective challengers had been working for nearly two and a half years on a close time table to be ready for a match in September of that year, and that a twelve months' postponement would be very costly for them besides creating "the greatest difficulties in keeping their crews together."

The Royal Thames challenge arrived in New York on October 17, less than a month after the conclusion of the prolonged *Weatherly-Gretel* proceedings at Newport. It was abruptly rejected the next day without explanation. New York saw no necessity for one. It had already made its position clear to all those concerned.

The quick turn-down rather shook the Londoners and so badly did it upset Anthony Bowden, who had engaged to build a challenge candidate from David Boyd's designs, that he made the following statement to an Associated Press correspondent: "The committee (Royal Thames) has examined the rules and, as I understand it, the position was that the Americans do not have the right to turn down a challenge. Under the deed of gift relating to the Cup they have to accept a challenge or else give up the Cup to the challenging club. . . . Perhaps the Americans have some grounds for postponing a challenge which we don't know about."

Mr. Boyden, who must have been talking strictly for home consumption, made himself look ridiculous on two counts:

1. Nowhere in the deed of gift is there anything which even by the greatest stretch of imagination compels a club holding the Cup to accept a challenge or forfeit the trophy.

2. There were no grounds for postponing a challenge which Mr. Boyden and all of the other brass at Royal Thames did not know about, and had not known ever since mid-September.

The Times of London took note of the situation about this time with an editorial leader which said:

The American rejection of the British challenge for the America's Cup has caused considerable disappointment in yachting circles. The New York Yacht Club are understood to have made their refusal on the grounds that to defend the Cup in two successive years would involve those taking part too great an expense and loss of time. It has also been suggested that too many challenges might tend to deprive the Cup of some of the prestige it holds at the present. At the same time it has been made clear that to postpone the contest until 1964 would be a serious blow to British

In a close race to windward, the trailing boat is always under pressure to keep her wind clear. These two pictures show how it is done. In the first photograph, Nefertiti has just tacked on Columbia's wind so Skipper Glit Shields quickly spins his vessel about. (Note how Columbia's jib is still coming across the foredeck as her winchmen grind away.) In the second picture, Columbia has filled away on the new tack and is sailing across Nefertiti's wake. Even if Nefertiti comes around to be on the same tack with Columbia, the latter will have her nose out in clear air.

hopes. Crews, it is pointed out, cannot be kept in training indefinitely and neither they nor the owners can spare the time for serious match racing season after season. Moreover the Americans would have two years instead of one to design and build possible new defenders and thus the British, if they were not to be left behind, would have to begin the whole costly and laborious business of tank testing and designing all over again.

The British claim that they were given an assurance in 1960 that a challenge would be acceptable in 1963. For their part the Americans are firmly insisting that they are not bound to accept a challenge for any particular year. The argument that under the deed of gift the Americans had to accept a challenge or else give up the Cup to the challenging club should not be taken too seriously. No one would wish to see the Cup won from America, if that ever happens, other than fairly and squarely in a contest embarked upon willingly by both sides.

A few days after New York's rejection of the challenge became public, another cable was received from Mountbatten. It said: "Royal Thames Yacht Club regret challenge rejected before receipt of my letter on receipt of which we hope you will reconsider your decision failing which we challenge for September 1964. If you insist on 1964 request your agreement to release contents of my letter to press who keep asking for it."

New York's trustees thereupon convened on October 22, read the Earl's letter of October 17 and cable of the nineteenth, and accepted the challenge for a match in 12-Meter yachts in September 1964. It also agreed to the release of Mountbatten's letter and accompanied this agreement

with the announcement that it would simultaneously release the full text of the May 12, 1960, letter from the New York Yacht Club to the Royal Thames. New York was perfectly willing to let the public decide the merits of the squabble.

It won instant and whole-hearted support for its stand, many of the writers feeling that the English club had put New York in the embarrassing position of having to reject publicly a challenge after it had made plain to Royal Thames officials in private conversations that it would be impracticable if not impossible to put on another America's Cup show only a year after the Australian spectacle.

Ian Proctor, writing in the London *Daily Telegraph*, summed up very neatly the attitude of those English yachtsmen not directly involved in what he regarded as an unfortunate contretemps.

He emphasized that the Americans "had made no secret of the fact that they wanted a breather before any more America's Cup sailings," pointed out that they had "been extremely generous and sporting antagonists, never officially questioning the right of the challengers to have sails—those all-important factors in the yacht's performance—made in the U.S. instead of the country from which the challenger hailed," and then warned that "there would be little satisfaction in forcing such sportsmen to a weakened defence."

He looked at both sides of the controversy with this concluding statement: "The challengers have justifiable reason for wanting to race in 1963; the defenders have equally valid ones for wishing to postpone until 1964."

Proctor's article and that in the "Thunderer" put a period to expressions of English dissatisfaction—in public at any rate—and there were no further recriminations, official or otherwise. Thereafter all hands settled down to the job of preparing for the match. At least they did in England. Steps lagged across the Atlantic; it took Americans a long time to arouse themselves to the fact that another challenge match was in the near offing and something had to be done about it.

The Boyden yacht, built from plans drawn by *Sceptre*'s designer after extensive tank testing at the Stevens Institute in Hoboken and a good, long look at *Weatherly* and *Gretel* at Newport in and out of the water, was launched at Sandbank, Scotland, on July 6, 1963. She was christened *Sovereign* as she slid into the waters of Holy Loch.

First to her dimensions: length overall 69 feet, waterline 46½ feet, beam 12½ feet, draft 9 feet, displacement 60,000 pounds, sail area 1,870. In contrast to *Sceptre*'s buxom entrance, *Sovereign* has a sharp entering edge to her keel. Her topsides flare slightly and her stern has the reverse slope of *Columbia* and *Gretel*. Like *Weatherly* and *Gretel, Sovereign* has an unraked rectangular rudder which contributes to her lateral plane. The stern is wide and powerful and her after-sections show a good flat run. Experts who have inspected her in and out of the water feel that David Boyd, after his sessions in the towing tank

with various models, learned a great deal that he never had an opportunity to find out with *Sceptre*. Thus *Sovereign* in many respects appears to have the attributes which Payne incorporated in *Gretel* and which showed in a slightly lesser degree in *Columbia*. The wedge-shaped bottom of *Columbia*'s lead, a feature of her 1962 changes, is seen in *Sovereign*, too.

Sovereign's rig looked clean and efficient to those who saw her sailing early trials against *Sceptre*, but they had some misgivings about her finely tapered aluminum spar which had two sets of spreaders but no jumper struts. Late in her first summer, *Sovereign* lost that mast overside. Once shaken down, *Sovereign* had no trouble with *Sceptre* and she did well against three old Twelves on the Solent.

On the basis of her performances through her short first season, it appears that *Sovereign* is much more of a boat than *Sceptre*, as indeed she would have to be to pose any sort of a threat to New York's Cup tenure. Those who are supposed to know about such things said she had a fine racing potential which could be realized with the right crew, a first-rate helmsman, and good management. Boyden thought so highly of *Sovereign* despite some British press criticism of his operating methods that he talked of building another Twelve to race against her because the old boats simply were not good enough to bring out her best.

Boyd had a set of plans for another boat, prepared at the same time that he was working on *Sovereign*'s lines. This

was the Twelve which the cognoscenti expected Erik Maxwell, *Sceptre*'s owner, and a group of associates, would build to rival Boyden's boat for the challenger's berth.

It was built—work began early in the fall of 1963—but not for Maxwell, nor for Boyden. Through a most unusual British-Australian cooperative effort her hull was being built for Frank and John Livingston, Melbourne cattle and sheep breeders, turf enthusiasts, and offshore racing yachtsmen. When ready for launching, she was to be turned over to Owen Aisher to be fitted out, manned and managed by him for the Royal Thames Yacht Club.

The Livingston-Aisher yacht was named *Kurrewa V* after a succession of successful Livingston-owned cruising boats, and was built in the same yard (Alexander Robertson and Sons at Sandbank, Argyll) which produced *Sceptre* and *Sovereign*.

Aisher has been mentioned as a possible challenger ever

⚓

Columbia *(1899 and 1901), the only yacht to defend twice. She defeated Sir Thomas Lipton's first two* Shamrocks.

⚓

Shamrock I, *first of the five green-hulled vessels of that name which the Scotch-Irish tea merchant, who became a baronet, was to send on unsuccessful quests for the Cup between 1899 and 1930.*

since the Twelves came into the picture. He has wide racing experience in 6-Meters, 5.5-Meters, cruising yachts, and formerly owned the prewar Twelve, *Evaine*, which was *Sceptre*'s trial horse in 1958. He is an amiable, good-humored, middle-aged man with two sailing sons and an intensely practical, hard-headed approach to the problems of major league yachting. Americans who know him believe that he will make *Kurrewa V* a very difficult boat for *Sovereign* to rule, if indeed, she does.

After the 1963 summer campaign, Boyden made some acquisitions for *Sovereign*'s afterguard which international sailing enthusiasts felt were bound to help her cause. He signed on Maxwell, who has done a great deal of 12-Meter racing; Bruce Banks, a young sailmaker with a local reputation for being able to make boats go; and Peter Scott, a yachting statesman who heads the International Yacht Racing Union. From this trio Boyden expected to appoint his Number One and relief helmsmen, and a navigator-tactician. Scott, a champion in dinghies and small boats in the thirties, and a Royal Navy motor torpedo boat hero in World War II, is considered the strongest bet for the post of tactical advisor and navigator.

Kurrewa V's skipper will be Colonel "Stug" Perry, an old friend and racing rival in the 6-Meter and 5.5-Meter classes. Aisher said of Perry on a visit to the United States in 1963: "He's a first-rate helmsman. I should know; he's beaten me often enough." *Kurrewa V*'s navigator, relief

helmsman and tactician will be Major General Ralph Farrant, a crack dinghy racer and offshore sailor.

The 1964 challenge will be historic if for no other reasons than it marks the first time in Cup annals that the British had two contemporaries as candidates for the challenger's role and made the final choice between them in American waters. They were scheduled to hold their preliminary trials off England's south coast in late spring and early summer, and then be shipped to the United States in July to resume their strife off Newport where the Cup match itself will be sailed.

In October 1963, a syndicate organized by two Oyster Bay, L.I., yachtsmen, Walter S. Gubelmann and Eric Ridder, let a contract to the Minneford Yacht Yard of City Island, N.Y., for the building of a Twelve from designs by Olin J. Stephens, *Columbia*'s creator. Stephens was ready. For some time he had been doing research and model testing at Stevens Institute on a grant from Briggs S. Cunningham, *Columbia*'s 1958 skipper. Although Cunningham had only tentatively thought about building a Twelve for himself, he felt that development within the class formula should proceed.

Cunningham was one of the first recruited for the syndicate which Gubelmann and Ridder, New York Yacht Club members, longtime friends and shipmates on Gubelmann's 71-foot ocean-racing yawl *Windigo*, christened *Constellation*. When the former Connecticut sportsman now living in

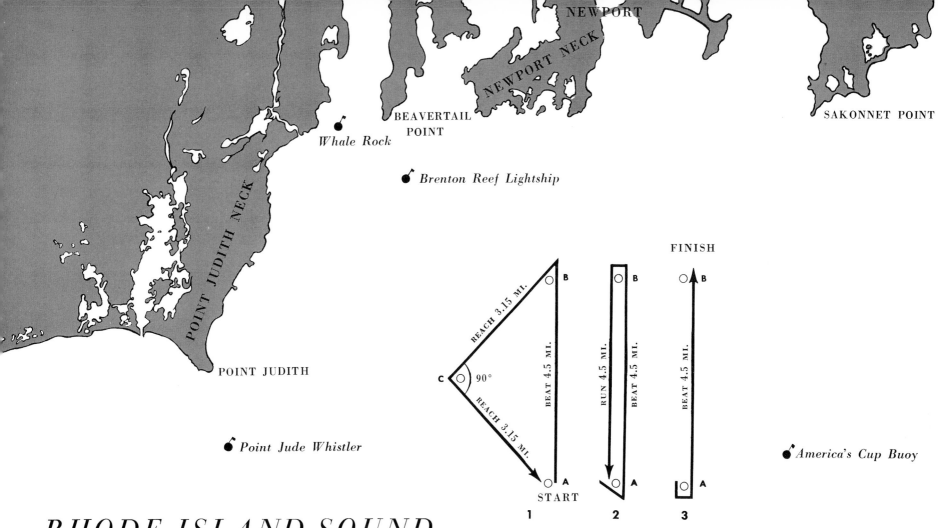

NEWPORT

NEWPORT NECK

SAKONNET POINT

BEAVERTAIL
POINT

Whale Rock

Brenton Reef Lightship

POINT JUDITH NECK

FINISH

B

REACH 3.15 MI.

BEAT 4.5 MI.

RUN 4.5 MI.

BEAT 4.5 MI.

BEAT 4.5 MI.

C 90°

POINT JUDITH

REACH 3.15 MI.

A

America's Cup Buoy

Point Jude Whistler

START

1   2   3

RHODE ISLAND SOUND

Outer Torpedo Range Bell

*Generally the trials to select the challenger are sailed off Brenton
Reef; the final Cup races take place some ten miles out to sea, near
the America's Cup Buoy and the Outer Torpedo Range Bell in
triangular, windward-leeward courses.*

*Starting in 1964, an Olympic course of 24.3 miles in the four-of-
seven Cup series will be sailed from a buoy nine miles south-south-
east of Brenton Reef Light. The course consists of six legs, as
outlined above. The time limit for each race is six hours.*

BLOCK ISLAND

Southern California, joined the group he turned over to it all of the results of Stephens' earlier research. Another member of the syndicate is none other than Harold S. Vanderbilt, who won the three Class J matches with *Enterprise*, *Rainbow*, and *Ranger* in the Thirties, and was a member of the selection committee which picked *Columbia* to meet *Sceptre* in 1958.

Ridder is to be skipper of the new boat which will be given the name *Constellation*. Robert N. Bavier, of Darien, Connecticut, a small boat helmsman of note and an experienced offshore racer, was named relief helmsman. The deck crew was built around Leo F. (Buddy) Bombard, who sailed with Bus Mosbacher in *Vim* and *Weatherly*; Larry Scheu, another *Vim* sailor; Richard Goennel, a top offshore racing hand who even has square-rigger experience in his log, and Fred Kulick, a young man who has been in *Windigo* three seasons. Gubelmann is the syndicate manager and K. Dun Gifford, the navigator.

For a trial horse, the Gubelmann-Ridder syndicate signed on *Nereus*, *Columbia*'s old playmate. This prewar 12-Meter was overhauled thoroughly at the Luders yard in Stamford, Connecticut, and, to make her more competitive, was fitted with one of the two sets of aluminum spars built for the first new American boat for the 1964 defense trials.

A month after the *Constellation* syndicate went into action, Pierre S. duPont III, Chesapeake Bay and Fishers Island yachtsman, revealed that he had organized a group to finance a Twelve designed by A. E. (Bill) Luders, Stamford naval architect and yacht yard operator. Lofting got underway immediately at the Luders plant—in anticipation of the order, Bill had basic plans ready and had rounded up many of the craftsmen who built *Weatherly* on the same ways in 1958.

As skipper, the duPont group has William S. Cox of Darien, Connecticut, a first-rate small-boat helmsman and catamaran enthusiast with an imposing list of national and Long Island Sound championships. Luders, who is regarded as one of the world's leading designers in the International Rule classes, made many contributions to the rehabilitation of *Weatherly* in 1962 and has been experimenting on 12-Meter hull designs for five years.

Both syndicates replaced *Rainbow*'s as the largest in Cup defense history. Their lists of contributors numbered thirty each. Eighteen persons, four of them Vanderbilts, financed the 1934 defender.

For a time in the autumn of 1963 it appeared that a third new Twelve would materialize. Homer R. Denius, a Florida cruising yachtsman and electronics research executive, attempted to organize an all-Florida syndicate to underwrite a Twelve designed by Charles Morgan, a young St. Petersburg sailmaker and developing naval architect, who had sailed in *Columbia*'s afterguard in the 1962 trials.

The project progressed far enough for Morgan to complete towing tank tests on two quite different models. Then

A. E. (Bill) Luders, Jr., of Stamford, Conn., has designed, built and raced yachts of the 6- and 5.5-Meter Classes since he produced his famous Totem in 1930. He began work on 12-Meter plans in 1957 and the lines and rig of the Aurora *syndicate Twelve are the culmination of these many years of research, observation, and tank testing. Many of his ideas and suggestions went into making* Weatherly *a winner in 1962.*

193

complications arose, most of them financial, and Denius decided that rather than do a hasty, last-minute job in 1964 he would concentrate on getting ready in all respects for the next defense trials, three years away, if this British challenge is turned back.

Would the old boats (they would be six years of age in 1964) have another try? No one had all of the answers. The Hovey family had a new narrow spreader rig like *Weatherly*'s built for *Easterner* and ordered several new sails. Ostensibly the family's plans for their yacht include sailing only for family fun. The only racing scheduled is the New York Yacht Club cruise. It will surprise no one, though if *Easterner* appears as a defense candidate for the third time. Her new rig, permitting greater area in the fore triangle, should make her livelier in light going and the narrow spreaders will make it possible to trim the genoas flatter and thus improve her weatherliness.

Columbia was put on the market after the death of her most recent owner, Paul V. Shields, but a high price tag discouraged prospective purchasers. The estate sought a quarter of a million. The best offer was reported to be $150,000, the sum for which she was sold by the syndicate which financed her winning 1958 campaign. A good deal of money was spent on her in 1961 and 1962.

Nefertiti, the only boat built especially for the 1962 defense, proved herself a powerful brute in heavy going and a very fast reacher. She has undergone changes which her designer-skipper-sailmaker, Ted Hood, expects will improve her speed in the lower ranges of the Beaufort scale. The keel was changed in size and form, her mainsail area increased and fore triangle commensurately reduced. The revisions were made in the hope of giving her more balanced performance. Only racing will reveal whether her Boston Yacht Club owners were justified in giving the big white boat another chance.

Weatherly is the biggest question of the 1958 trio. After she conquered *Gretel*, her owners, Henry D. Mercer, Cornelius Walsh and Arnold Frese, decided that she had earned retirement. She sat alongside *Columbia* and *Easterner* in the Luders yard the winter of 1963–1964 awaiting a decision on her future. Given the same skipper and crew she had in 1962, she would make a perfect yardstick by which to measure the new boats and to throw some light on whether the changes in *Nefertiti* had improved her light weather capability.

The fact is, though, that *Weatherly*'s owners could not stand seeing her beaten as it seems reasonable to expect she would be if our designers have profited by their experiences and studies of the last two years. And Mosbacher has been emphatic about being unavailable for America's Cup duty this time. He says he will be a spectator, not a participant, and he means it. He declined two commands.

A LOOK BACK

Cup Competition in Retrospect

The year 1881 was notable in America's Cup annals for several reasons, all of them firsts.

For the first time, the yacht named by the New York Yacht Club to face a challenger had to earn the honor by defeating other aspirants in a series of trials.

The schooner phase of Cup competition ended and the sloop era began when Canada sent the first single-masted vessel to the international yachting wars.

The year also marked the first time a boat was built especially for the defense, and by a syndicate rather than an individual. The fact that this yacht did not make the grade is of no moment. She established a precedent and a fashion—since her day every challenge has inspired the building of at least one new defense candidate and most have been financed by groups of yachtsmen organized for that purpose.

Until 1881 there had been no such formality as the holding of eliminations to decide what yacht was going to defend the Cup; New York's brass merely looked over the club racing squadron and assigned it either in toto or units to cope with the invader.

James Ashbury, who carried out the first two challenges under the white ensign of the Royal Yacht Squadron, learned to his distress how determined New York was to retain in its possession the 100-guinea Squadron Cup which *America* had won by defeating fourteen British adversaries in a race around the Isle of Wight on August 22, 1851.

When Ashbury sailed *Cambria* over here from England in 1870 (he won a transatlantic match from the American schooner *Dauntless* in the process), the Britisher was required to race twenty-three New York Yacht Club schooners for the Cup. *Cambria* finished tenth, rather a noteworthy performance in view of the fact that, as individuals, her massed opposition was not so much interested in winning the race as it was bent on preventing *Cambria* from taking the prize back to Britain.

A year later, when Ashbury returned with the schooner *Livonia*, New York had relented somewhat, but by no means to the point that a fair match had been set up. However, instead of having her race the whole fleet, it was arranged for *Livonia* to tackle only four yachts, one at a time, New York reserving the right to name the defender for that day just before the start of any race. In those unenlightened times such a disposition of forces against a challenger was considered, by the host club at least, to be quite a sporting gesture.

As things turned out, New York used only two boats, the light weather speed queen *Columbia*, a centerboarder, and the keel schooner *Sappho*, which was at her best in heavy going. *Palmer* and *Dauntless* sat it out.

There were no problems when it came time to pick a defender to meet the Royal Canadian Yacht Club's schooner *Countess of Dufferin*. Before the 1876 competition, it had been agreed to make it a match, that is, one boat against one and no shenanigans such as the deal *Livonia* bought. The fastest two-master in the United States was John Stiles Dickerson's *Madeleine*. She could, and did, conquer all of the others with regularity and decisiveness. Without a second thought, she was assigned to the defense task, an action which she justified by defeating the Canadian by awesome margins.

A third generation of Dickersons, incidentally, is carrying on the family's Cup tradition. John S. Dickerson, Jr., grandson of *Madeleine*'s owner, was chairman of the race committee which presided over the *Columbia-Sceptre* series. His brother, W. Mahlon Dickerson, was secretary of the 1962 America's Cup committee and is now rear commodore of the New York Yacht Club.

The first yacht built expressly as a Cup defense candidate was the 72-foot centerboard sloop *Pocahontas*, which was quickly rechristened "Pokey" by irreverent observers of her sailing qualities. When Canada's Bay of Quinte Yacht Club challenged on behalf of *Atalanta*, the first single-sticker to have a try at America's trophy, New York's flag officers surveyed the few large sloops in their fleet and decided something newer and faster was indicated.

They commissioned David Kirby, *Madeleine*'s creator, to produce such a vessel. They could have saved their money. The boat he turned out from a whittled model—naval architecture in those days was a relatively uncomplicated

science—was absolutely no match for two older craft, *Mischief* and *Gracie*. After three races, *Mischief* was picked as defender. The three commodores, James R. Waller, James D. Smith, and Herman Oelrichs, took their disappointment philosophically and forthwith converted *Pocahontas* into a cruising yacht.

Gracie's owners, Charles R. Flint and Joseph P. Earle, reacted quite differently. They took an extremely dim view of *Mischief*'s selection after she had beaten *Gracie* only fourteen seconds in the third match (each had won once previously), and proceeded through correspondence with newspapers to let the public know what they thought of the committee's judgment. Then, when *Mischief* raced *Atalanta*, they took leave of their sailing manners and went around the course with the contestants.

The Canadian was widely outclassed. *Mischief* trounced her by 28 minutes in their first meeting and 39 in the sec-

⚓

An unforgettable moment in yachting history and one which won't be repeated in our time. Five of the 135-foot Class J sloops with their 160-foot masts hitting the starting line in a New York Yacht Club cruise race in 1937 after Ranger *had demolished* Endeavour II's *hopes. Reading from left to right, or from windward to leeward,* Endeavour I, Rainbow, Ranger, Endeavour II, Yankee. *Only* Endeavour II *has not been shattered by a shipbreaker's hammer.*

ond. Simultaneously, *Mischief* proved to be 6 minutes 27 seconds slower than *Gracie* in the opening test and 4:38 faster in the next.

Contrast the attitude of *Gracie*'s owners with that of the *Yankee* syndicate in 1934. After blowing out a genoa jib while leading on the windward leg of the fifth race of the final trials that summer, *Yankee* was beaten only one second by *Rainbow* and, that evening, passed over for selection. Bostonian disappointment was keen. *Yankee* adherents felt that since two of *Rainbow*'s three victories in the final trials were the direct result of mishaps on *Yankee*, the New England boat should have had another chance.

There was no irresponsible complaining in the press, though, and when *Rainbow* got into trouble with *Endeavour*, *Yankee*'s designer and light sails expert, Frank C. Paine, stepped aboard *Rainbow* with *Yankee*'s exceptionally fine spinnaker and helped the embattled defender to defeat the Britisher.

Cup defenders appear seven times on the list of yachts which have failed of selection. This is explained by the fact that subsequent to their Cup victories they returned as trial horses for new boats, or as serious candidates for another nomination. Only one, the second *Columbia*, was tapped twice.

She turned back Sir Thomas Lipton's first challenger in 1899 and was chosen two years later to face *Shamrock II*. She achieved this distinction by defeating in the trials the boat which had been built to beat her, *Constitution*. In 1903, *Columbia* tried for a third time, but in this instance the Wizard of Bristol, Nathanael Greene Herreshoff, definitely had improved on her. *Columbia* and *Constitution* were solidly beaten by *Reliance*, a huge overcanvassed skimming dish, which was so extreme that she brought about a change in construction rules aimed at producing a more wholesome type of racing yacht.

Another *Columbia*, third of the name and first of the new International 12-Meter Class yachts built for the 1958 defense, was twice a candidate. She was selected to race *Sceptre* that year, but in 1962 was outsailed by *Weatherly*, one of the boats she had defeated four years earlier.

APPENDICES

Appendix I. THE AMERICA'S CUP RECORD

DATE	COURSE	DEFENDER	TIME	CHALLENGER	TIME	SCORE
1870						
Aug. 8	NYYC,* 35.1 miles	Magic	3:38:26	Cambria	4:37:38	U.S. 1–0 †
1871						
Oct. 16	NYYC, 35.1 miles	Columbia	6:19:41	Livonia	6:46:45	
Oct. 18	40 miles, windward-leeward	Columbia	3:07:42	Livonia	3:18:15	
Oct. 19	NYYC, 35.1 miles	Columbia	4:17:35	Livonia	4:02:25	
Oct. 21	40 miles, windward-leeward	Sappho	5:36:02	Livonia	6:09:23	
Oct. 23	NYYC, 40 miles	Sappho	4:46:17	Livonia	5:11:44	U.S. 4–1 **
1876						
Aug. 11	NYYC, 32.6 miles	Madeleine	5:23:54	Countess of Dufferin	5:34:53	
Aug. 12	40 miles, windward-leeward	Madeleine	7:18:46	Countess of Dufferin	7:46:00	U.S. 2–0
1881						
Nov. 9	NYYC, 32.6 miles	Mischief	4:17:09	Atalanta	4:45:29	
Nov. 10	32 miles, leeward-windward	Mischief	4:54:53	Atalanta	5:33:47	U.S. 2–0
1885						
Sept. 14	NYYC, 32.6 miles	Puritan	6:06:05	Genesta	6:22:24	
Sept. 16	40 miles, leeward-windward	Puritan	5:03:14	Genesta	5:04:52	U.S. 2–0
1886						
Sept. 9	NYYC, 32.6 miles	Mayflower	5:26:41	Galatea	5:38:43	
Sept. 11	40 miles, leeward-windward	Mayflower	6:49:00	Galatea	7:18:09	U.S. 2–0

1887						
Sept. 27	NYYC, 32.6 miles	Volunteer	4:53:18	Thistle	5:12:41	
Sept. 30	40 miles, windward-leeward	Volunteer	5:42:56	Thistle	5:54:45	U.S. 2–0
1893						
Oct. 7	30 miles, windward-leeward	Vigilant	4:05:47	Valkyrie II	4:11:35	
Oct. 9	30 miles, triangular	Vigilant	3:25:01	Valkyrie II	3:35:36	
Oct. 13	30 miles, windward-leeward	Vigilant	3:24:39	Valkyrie II	3:25:19	U.S. 3–0
1895						
Sept. 7	30 miles, windward-leeward	Defender	4:59:55	Valkyrie III	5:08:44	
Sept. 10	30 miles, triangular	Defender	3:55:56	Valkyrie III	Disqualified	
Sept. 12	30 miles, leeward-windward	Defender	4:43:43	Valkyrie III	Withdrew	U.S. 3–0
1899						
Oct. 16	30 miles, windward-leeward	Columbia	4:53:53	Shamrock I	5:04:07	
Oct. 17	30 miles, triangular	Columbia	3:37:00	Shamrock I	Disabled	
Oct. 20	30 miles, leeward-windward	Columbia	3:38:09	Shamrock I	3:44:43	U.S. 3–0
1901						
Sept. 28	30 miles, windward-leeward	Columbia	4:30:24	Shamrock II	4:31:44	
Oct. 3	30 miles, triangular	Columbia	3:12:35	Shamrock II	3:16:10	
Oct. 4	30 miles, leeward-windward	Columbia	4:32:57	Shamrock II	4:33:38	U.S. 3–0
1903						
Aug. 22	30 miles, windward-leeward	Reliance	3:32:17	Shamrock III	3:39:20	
Aug. 25	30 miles, triangular	Reliance	3:14:54	Shamrock III	3:16:12	
Sept. 3	30 miles, leeward-windward	Reliance	4:28:00	Shamrock III	Lost in fog	U.S. 3–0

* The New York Yacht Club (NYYC) course was fixed in New York harbor and was not altered to meet daily weather variations.

† *Cambria* raced against New York Yacht Club fleet of 23 schooners. *Magic* won, *America* was fourth, and *Cambria* tenth.

** *Livonia* raced against *Columbia* and *Sappho* on different days because New York Yacht Club reserved the right to name the defender before each race, basing its selection on the prevailing weather. *Livonia* won the second race when *Columbia* finished disabled.

Appendix I. THE AMERICA'S CUP RECORD (continued)

DATE	COURSE	DEFENDER	TIME	CHALLENGER	TIME	SCORE
1920						
July 15	30 miles, windward-leeward	Resolute	Disabled	Shamrock IV	4:24:58	
July 20	30 miles, triangular	Resolute	5:24:44	Shamrock IV	5:22:18	
July 21	30 miles, windward-leeward	Resolute	3:56:05	Shamrock IV	4:03:06	
July 23	30 miles, triangular	Resolute	3:31:12	Shamrock IV	3:41:10	
July 27	30 miles, windward-leeward	Resolute	5:28:35	Shamrock IV	5:48:20	U.S. 3–2
1930						
Sept. 13	30 miles, leeward-windward	Enterprise	4:03:48	Shamrock V	4:06:40	
Sept. 15	30 miles, triangular	Enterprise	4:00:44	Shamrock V	4:10:18	
Sept. 17	30 miles, windward-leeward	Enterprise	3:54:16	Shamrock V	Disabled	
Sept. 18	30 miles, triangular	Enterprise	3:10:13	Shamrock V	3:15:57	U.S. 4–0
1934						
Sept. 17	30 miles, windward-leeward	Rainbow	3:45:53	Endeavour	3:43:44	
Sept. 18	30 miles, triangular	Rainbow	3:09:52	Endeavour	3:09:01	
Sept. 20	30 miles, leeward-windward	Rainbow	4:35:34	Endeavour	4:39:00	
Sept. 22	30 miles, triangular	Rainbow	3:15:38	Endeavour	3:16:53	
Sept. 24	30 miles, leeward-windward	Rainbow	3:54:05	Endeavour	3:58:06	
Sept. 25	30 miles, triangular	Rainbow	3:40:05	Endeavour	3:41:00	U.S. 4–2
1937						
July 31	30 miles, windward-leeward	Ranger	4:41:15	Endeavour II	4:58:20	
Aug. 2	30 miles, triangular	Ranger	3:41:33	Endeavour II	4:00:05	
Aug. 4	30 miles, windward-leeward	Ranger	3:54:30	Endeavour II	3:58:57	
Aug. 5	30 miles, triangular	Ranger	3:07:49	Endeavour II	3:11:26	U.S. 4–0

1958						
Sept. 20	24 miles, windward-leeward	Columbia	5:13:56	Sceptre	5:21:41	
Sept. 24	24 miles, triangular	Columbia	3:17:42	Sceptre	3:29:24	
Sept. 25	24 miles, windward-leeward	Columbia	3:09:07	Sceptre	3:17:27	
Sept. 26	24 miles, triangular	Columbia	3:04:22	Sceptre	3:11:27	U.S. 4–0
1962						
Sept. 15	24 miles, windward-leeward	Weatherly	3:13:57	Gretel	3:17:43	
Sept. 18	24 miles, triangular	Weatherly	2:47:45	Gretel	2:46:48	
Sept. 20	24 miles, windward-leeward	Weatherly	4:21:16	Gretel	4:29:56	
Sept. 22	24 miles, triangular	Weatherly	3:22:28	Gretel	3:22:54	
Sept. 25	24 miles, windward-leeward	Weatherly	3:16:17	Gretel	3:19:57	U.S. 4–1

NOTE: From 1870 through 1920 the races were held with time allowances based on varying measurement formulae.

The matches of 1930, '34 and '37 were sailed in yachts of the 76-rating Class J sloops built to the Universal rule, without time allowance.

The matches of 1958 and 1962 were in yachts of the International 12-Meter Class, and, as in the three previous contests, without time allowance.

Up to and including the *Resolute-Shamrock IV* match of 1920, all races were held either over the so-called New York Yacht Club course in New York Bay or off Sandy Hook. Beginning with 1930, all matches were sailed from a starting point 9 miles southeast of Brenton Reef Lightvessel off Newport, R. I.

Atalanta and the *Countess of Dufferin* were Canadian; *Gretel* was Australia's first challenger. All of the others were from the United Kingdom.

Atalanta was the first sloop to challenge for the Cup. Previously the prize had been contested in schooners. From 1881 all matches were sailed in single-masted yachts.

Resolute (1920) was the last gaff-headed defender. When the J boats came into vogue in 1930 so did the Marconi or jib-headed mainsail.

Appendix II. *YACHTS' VITAL STATISTICS*

DATE	YACHT	DESIGNER	BUILDER	LENGTH OVERALL	LENGTH AT WATER LINE	BEAM	DRAFT	TONS	SAIL AREA (IN FEET)	SKIPPER
1851	America	George Steers	W. H. Brown	101'9"	96'6"	22'6"	11'	170.5	5,253	Richard Brown
1870	Magic	R. F. Loper	T. Byerly & Son	84'	79'	20'9"	6'3" *	92.2	1,680 †	Andrew J. Comstock
	Cambria	Michael Ratsey	Michael Ratsey	108'	98'	21'	12'	248	2,106	J. Linnock
1871	Columbia	J. B. van Dusen	J. B. van Dusen	107'10"	96'5"	25'6"	5'11" *	230		Nelson Comstock
	Sappho	C. & R. Poillon	C. & R. Poillon	135'	119'4"	27'4"	12'8"	310	7,060	Sam Greenwood
	Livonia	Michael Ratsey	Michael Ratsey	127'2"	106'2"	23'7"	12'6"	280	8,153	J. R. Woods
1876	Madeleine	David Kirby	David Kirby	106'4"	95'	24'3"	7'3" *	151.5		Josephus Williams
	Countess of Dufferin	Alex Cuthbert	Alex Cuthbert	107'		24'	6'6" *	138.2		Alex Cuthbert / Capt. J. Ellsworth
1881	Mischief	A. Cary Smith	Harlan & Hollingsworth	67'5"	61'	19'10"	5'4" *	79.2		Nathaniel Clock
	Atalanta	Alex Cuthbert	Alex Cuthbert	70'	64'	19'	5'6" *	84		Alex Cuthbert
1885	Puritan	Edw. Burgess	Lawley	94'	81'1"	22'7"	8'8" *	140	7,982	Aubrey Crocker
	Genesta	Beavor Webb	Beavor Webb	90'	81'	15'	13'6"	80	7,150	John Carter
1886	Mayflower	Edw. Burgess	Edw. Burgess	100'	85'6"	23'6"	9'9" *	171.7	8,500	Martin V. B. Stone
	Galatea	Beavor Webb	J. Reed & Son	102'7"	86'10"	15'	13'6"	171.1	7,751	Dan Bradford
1887	Volunteer	Edw. Burgess	Pusey & Jones	106'3"	85'10"	23'2"	10' *	209	9,271	Henry C. Haff
	Thistle	G. L. Watson	D. & W. Henderson & Co.	108'6"	86'5"	20'3"	13'10"	253.9	8,968	John Barr
1893	Vigilant	N. G. Herreshoff	N. G. Herreshoff	124'	86'	26'3"	14' *		11,242	Wm. Hansen
	Valkyrie II	G. L. Watson	G. L. Watson	117'3"	85'10"	22'4"	16'		10,042	Wm. Cranfield
1895	Defender	N. G. Herreshoff	N. G. Herreshoff	123'	88'5"	23'	19'		12,602	Henry C. Haff
	Valkyrie III	G. L. Watson	G. L. Watson	129'	88'10"	26'2"	20'		13,028	Wm. Cranfield

Year	Yacht	Designer	Builder							Skipper
1899	Columbia	N. G. Herreshoff	N. G. Herreshoff	131'	89'8"	24'	19'3"		13,135	Charles Barr
	Shamrock I	Wm. Fife, Jr.	Thorneycrofts	128'	89'8"	25'	20'3"		13,492	Archie Hogarth
1901	Columbia	N. G. Herreshoff	N. G. Herreshoff	131'	89'8"	24'	19'3"		13,135	Charles Barr
	Shamrock II	G. L. Watson	Wm. Denny & Brother	137'	89'3"	24'	20'		14,027	E. A. Sycamore
1903	Reliance	N. G. Herreshoff	N. G. Herreshoff	143'8"	89'8"	25'8"	20'		16,159	Charles Barr
	Shamrock III	Wm. Fife, Jr.	Wm. Fife, Jr.	134'	89'10"	23'	19'		14,154	R. Ringe
1920	Resolute	N. G. Herreshoff	N. G. Herreshoff	106'3"	74'10"	21'1"	13'8"		8,775	C. F. Adams
	Shamrock IV	C. E. Nicholson	Camper & Nicholson	110'3"	75'	22'2"	14'		10,459	W. T. Burton
1930	Enterprise	W. S. Burgess	Herreshoff	120'10"	80'	22'1"	14'7"	128	7,583	H. S. Vanderbilt
	Shamrock V	C. E. Nicholson	Camper & Nicholson	119'1"	81'1"	19'9"	14'9"	134	7,540	Ted Heard
1934	Rainbow	W. S. Burgess	Herreshoff	127'3"	82'	21'	14'7"	141.1	7,572	H. S. Vanderbilt
	Endeavour	C. E. Nicholson	Camper & Nicholson	129'8"	83'3"	22'	14'10"	143.1	7,561	T. O. M. Sopwith
1937	Ranger	W. S. Burgess & O. J. Stephens	Bath Iron Works	135'2"	87'	21'	15'	166	7,546	H. S. Vanderbilt
	Endeavour II	C. E. Nicholson	Camper & Nicholson	135'9"	87'	21'6"	15'	162.6	7,543	T. O. M. Sopwith
1958	Columbia	O. J. Stephens	Nevins	69'4"	46'2"	11'9"	9'	28.4	1,817	B. S. Cunningham
	Sceptre	David Boyd	Alex Robertson & Sons	68'10"	46'6"	11'9"	9'1"	29.7	1,819	Graham Mann
1962	Weatherly	P. L. Rhodes	Luders	66'9"	46'9"	11'3"	9'	30.5	1,845	E. Mosbacher, Jr.
	Gretel	Alan Payne	Halvorsen Brothers	69'6"	45'	11'1"	9'	29.6	1,854	Jock Sturrock

* Centerboard up.

† Lowers only.

NOTE: Where blanks appear under tonnage and sail area, figures do not appear in records. Until Class J era, beginning with *Enterprise* and *Shamrock V*, tonnage given is New York Customs House register. From 1930 onward, tonnage given is actual displacement.

Appendix III. DEFENDER AND CHALLENGER OWNERS

DATE	YACHT	OWNERS	CLUB
1851 *	America	Commodore John C. Stevens, Edwin A. Stevens, George L. Schuyler, Col. James A. Hamilton, Hamilton Wiles, John K. Beekman Finlay	New York Yacht Club
1870	Magic	Franklin Osgood	New York Yacht Club
	Cambria	James Ashbury	Royal Thames Yacht Club
1871	Columbia	Franklin Osgood	New York Yacht Club
	Sappho	Col. William L. Douglas	New York Yacht Club
	Livonia	James Ashbury	Royal Harwich Yacht Club
1876	Madeleine	John S. Dickerson	New York Yacht Club
	Countess of Dufferin	Major Charles Gifford, head of building syndicate	Royal Canadian Yacht Club
1881	Mischief	Joseph R. Busk	New York Yacht Club
	Atalanta	Alexander Cuthbert	Bay of Quinte Yacht Club
1885	Puritan	J. Malcolm Forbes, General Charles J. Paine, William Gray Jr., Henry S. Hovey, William F. Weld, Augustus Hemenway, W. H. Forbes, John L. Gardner, J. Montgomery Sears, F. L. Higginson	Eastern Yacht Club
	Genesta	Sir Richard Sutton	Royal Yacht Squadron
1886	Mayflower	General Charles J. Paine	New York Yacht Club
	Galatea	Lieut. William Henn, RN	Royal Northern Yacht Club
1887	Volunteer	General Charles J. Paine	New York Yacht Club
	Thistle	James Bell, John Clark, Andrew Clark, Andrew William, James and George Coates, J. Hilliard Bell, William Bell	Royal Clyde Yacht Club
1893	Vigilant	C. Oliver Iselin, Edwin D. Morgan, August Belmont, Oliver Belmont, Cornelius Vanderbilt, Charles R. Flint, Chester W. Chapin, George C. Clark, Henry Astor Cary, Dr. Barton Hopkins, E. M. Fulton, Jr.	New York Yacht Club
	Valkyrie II	The Earl of Dunraven, Wyndham Thomas-Wyndham Quin	Royal Yacht Squadron
1895	Defender	William K. Vanderbilt, E. D. Morgan, C. Oliver Iselin	New York Yacht Club
	Valkyrie III	Lord Dunraven, Lord Lonsdale, Lord Wolverton, Capt. Harry McCalmont	Royal Yacht Squadron
1899	Columbia	J. Pierpont Morgan, E. D. Morgan, C. Oliver Iselin	New York Yacht Club
	Shamrock I	Sir Thomas Lipton	Royal Ulster Yacht Club

208

1901	Columbia	J. Pierpont Morgan, E. D. Morgan	New York Yacht Club
	Shamrock II	Sir Thomas Lipton	Royal Ulster Yacht Club
1903	Reliance	Cornelius Vanderbilt, William Rockefeller, P. A. B. Widener, Elbert H. Gary, Clement A. Griscom, James J. Hill, W. B. Leeds, Norman B. Ream, Henry Walters	New York Yacht Club
	Shamrock III	Sir Thomas Lipton	Royal Ulster Yacht Club
1920	Resolute	Henry Walters, Cornelius Vanderbilt, J. P. Morgan, F. G. Bourne, George F. Baker, Jr., Arthur Curtiss James, H. S. Vanderbilt, Richard T. Crane, Payne Whitney	New York Yacht Club
	Shamrock IV	Sir Thomas Lipton	Royal Ulster Yacht Club
1930	Enterprise	Winthrop W. Aldrich, Vincent Astor, George F. Baker, Jr., Floyd L. Carlisle, E. H. Clark, Harold S. Vanderbilt, George Whitney	New York Yacht Club
	Shamrock V	Sir Thomas Lipton, Bart	Royal Ulster Yacht Club
1934	Rainbow	Harold S. Vanderbilt, F. W. Vanderbilt, W. K. Vanderbilt, A. G. Vanderbilt, J. P. Morgan, Gerard B. Lambert, Marshall Field, Edward S. Harkness, George F. Baker, Charles Hayden, George E. Roosevelt, W. G. McCullough, Joseph P. Day, H. H. Rogers, Walter P. Chrysler, Ogden P. Mills, Alfred P. Sloane, W. W. Aldrich	New York Yacht Club
	Endeavour	Thomas O. M. Sopwith	Royal Yacht Squadron
1937	Ranger	Harold S. Vanderbilt	New York Yacht Club
	Endeavour II	Thomas O. M. Sopwith	Royal Yacht Squadron
1958	Columbia	Henry Sears, Gerard B. Lambert, B. S. Cunningham, Vincent Astor, James A. Farrell, A. Howard Fuller, William T. Moore	New York Yacht Club
	Sceptre	Hugh Goodson, Viscount Runciman, H. A. Andreae, Bertram Currie, Group Capt. Lowell Guinness, Major H. W. Hall, Sir Peter Hoare, Major R. N. Macdonald-Buchanan, Charles G. C. Wainman, Viscount Camrose, Lt. Col. A. W. Ackland, Sir Joku Wardlaw-Milne	Royal Yacht Squadron
1962	Weatherly	Henry D. Mercer, Cornelius Walsh, Arnold D. Frese	New York Yacht Club
	Gretel	Sir Frank Packer, Richard Dickson, William H. Northam, William G. Walkley, Noel Foley	Royal Sydney Yacht Squadron

* *America* raced against a British fleet. The formal competition, between defender and challenger, began in 1870.

Appendix IV. CONTENDERS ELIMINATED IN TRIALS TO SELECT DEFENDERS

DATE	YACHT	DESIGNER [*]	SYNDICATE
1881	Pocahontas	David Kirby	New York Yacht Club Flag Officers' Syndicate: James R. Waller, James D. Smith, Herman Oelrichs
	Gracie	Polhemus of Nyack	Charles R. Flint, Joseph P. Earle
	Hildegard	A. E. Smith of Islip	Herman Oelrichs
1885	Priscilla	Archibald Cary Smith	James Gordon Bennett, William P. Douglas
	Bedouin	John Harvey	Archibald Rogers
	Gracie		
1886	Atlantic	Philip Ellsworth	Latham A. Fish, J. Rogers Maxwell, William Ziegler, Newbury D. Lawton *et al.*
	Puritan		Eastern Yacht Club Syndicate
	Priscilla		
1887	Mayflower		E. D. Morgan
1893	Colonia	N. G. Herreshoff	Archibald Rogers, Frederick W. Vanderbilt, William K. Vanderbilt, F. Augustus Schermerhorn, J. Pierpont Morgan, John E. Brooks
	Jubilee	Charles J. Paine John B. Paine	Charles J. Paine
	Pilgrim	Stewart & Binney	Bayard Thayer, William Amory Gardner, Charles H. Taylor *et al.*
1895	Vigilant		George J. Gould
1899	Defender		J. Pierpont Morgan, Butler Duncan
1901	Constitution	N. G. Herreshoff	August Belmont, James Stillman, Oliver H. Payne, F. G. Bourne, Henry Walters
	Independence	B. B. Crowninshield	Thomas W. Lawson
1903	Columbia	E. D. Morgan	
	Constitution		
1914–20 †	Defiance	George Owen	George M. Pynchon, E. Walter Clark *et al.*
	Vanitie	William Gardner	Alexander Cochran

1930	Whirlwind	L. Francis Herreshoff	Landon K. Thorpe, Paul L. Hammond, George M. Pynchon *et al.*
	Yankee	Frank C. Paine	John Lawrence, Frank C. Paine, Charles Francis Adams, Chandler Hovey, *et al.*
	Weetamoe	Clinton H. Crane	Junius S. Morgan, George Nichols *et al.*
1934	Weetamoe		Frederick H. Prince
	Yankee		Chandler Hovey, Charles Francis Adams *et al.*
1937	Rainbow		Chandler Hovey
	Yankee		Gerard B. Lambert
1958	Weatherly	Philip L. Rhodes	Henry D. Mercer, Arnold D. Frese, Cornelius Walsh
	Easterner	C. Raymond Hunt	Chandler Hovey
	Vim	Olin J. Stevens	John N. Matthews
1962	Easterner		
	Columbia		Paul V. Shields
	Nefertiti	Frederick E. Hood	E. Ross Anderson, Robert W. Purcell *et al.*

* In the early years the designer was actually the builder or "modeler."

† *Defiance* participated in 1914 trials before the match with *Shamrock IV* was postponed because of the outbreak in Europe of World War I. When the match was re-scheduled for 1920, only *Vanitie* raced against *Resolute* in the trials.

NOTE: Names of designers or syndicate owners are not repeated when boats appeared in previous trials, if there have been no changes.

GLOSSARY

The following explanations of yachting terms used in this book are intended to help those non-sailing readers to whom racing expressions are unfamiliar and therefore confusing.

Abaft Toward the stern; behind; aft of.

Backstays Wire stays which lead aft from the mast. The so-called *permanent backstay* runs from the masthead to the after deck or taffrail. *Backstay runners* or *running backstays* lead aft from the point on the mast where the *jibstay* (the wire on which the jib is set) is attached to positions on either side of the cockpit. When the boat is on the port tack the port *runner* (the weather *backstay*) is set up taut and the starboard *runner* (at this moment the leeward backstay) is slacked off and carried forward to keep it from chafing against the lee side of the mainsail. Whenever the boat is tacked, positions of *running backstays* have to be alternated. *Permanent backstay*, as the name implies, remains in place.

Beat To work to windward by alternate tacks. Starting in 1964, 13.5 miles—more than half the America's Cup course will be sailed to windward.

Board Not a plank in this case. A yacht takes, or sails, a long (or short) board on either starboard or port tack depending on which side she is carrying her main boom. She is on port tack when the wind is coming from the port side and the boom is to starboard; on starboard tack when these conditions are reversed.

Clearing tack A tack made for the purpose of clearing one's wind, that is, turning away from an opponent positioned so as to interfere with the clear flow of air to the other boat's sails.

Coffee grinder Sailors' name for a pedestal-type winch activated by rotating two handles affixed to opposite sides of the pedestal; normally used for heaviest work such as trimming jibs, spinnaker sheets, and guys.

Covering Maneuvering so as to maintain position between a trailing opponent and the next mark of the course.

Drifter A headsail made of very light fabric and used only in very light airs, that is, drifting conditions.

False tack The name applied to the maneuver that gives the appearance of coming about from one tack to another, in which a boat actually rolls back to the original tack after coming head to wind or close thereto; this technique is often resorted to by a boat trying to break away from an adversary covering her on the windward leg of the course.

Fetch(ing) A yacht is said to be fetching the windward mark when there is no doubt that its present course will take it to the buoy without another tack. Sometimes used as distance in this manner: "It is only a short *fetch* to the weather mark."

Fore triangle The area bounded by a yacht's mast, jibstay, and foredeck. The larger the fore triangle, the larger the jibs and spinnakers which may be used.

Hanks Clips used to attach jibs to the jibstay.

Header A shift of wind which makes it necessary for the boat to be steered at a less favorable angle to the windward mark; one, in other words, which knocks the boat's head off, or away from, the desired course.

Headsails All sails set forward of the mast and thus at head of the vessel, as opposed to its tail, or stern; includes jibs, staysails, and spinnakers.

Headstay Forward mast support; runs from head of mast to fitting on the bow.

Hitch In the sailing sense rather than marlinspike seamanship, a tack. A boat going to windward may have to make a short *hitch*, or tack, to be able to round or *fetch* a mark, or she may take a *hitch* inshore, or to the westward.

Jib numbers In yacht racing, overlapping, or Genoa, jibs are numbered according to size, No. 1 being the largest, No. 4 the smallest.

Jibe, jibing When sailing before the wind, that is, with the breeze astern or nearly so, a yacht jibes (carries out the act of jibing) when her stern is swung through the wind to bring the breeze from one quarter to the other and thus cause the boom to move across the deck to the side opposite to that on which it had been carried.

Kite Synonym for spinnaker, which is sometimes also referred to as a *bag*.

Laying, lay line A yacht is on the *lay line*, or *laying* the mark, when she is on the tack which will carry her to the windward mark provided no unforeseen wind shift causes her to fail to *fetch* on that tack, or badly *overstand*, that is, be further to windward than necessary.

Lee bow The side of the bow away from the wind; thus, a yacht *lee bows* another when it tacks in a position to leeward of and close to the windward yacht's bow.

Lift A line which runs from the forward side of the mast to approximately the middle of the spinnaker pole to help control its position with relation to the deck. Also, in sailing, a shift of wind which permits a yacht to sail a course closer to windward mark; the opposite of a *header*.

Luff The leading edge of a sail. In tactics, *luffing* is the act of sailing a boat as high as head to wind to prevent an overtaking yacht from passing to windward.

Off the wind Sailing free, that is with the wind fair rather than ahead; the opposite of "on the wind," or to windward.

Overlap An overlap exists between two yachts when neither is clear astern of the other, that is, when any part of the trailing yacht or its equipment is forward of an imaginary line drawn across the aftermost part of the leading boat at right angles to its centerline.

Pinching Sailing a boat too close to the wind, that is, pointing the boat's nose higher at the sacrifice of speed through the water.

Reacher Reaching jib; a jib shaped especially to give maximum performance when sailing across the wind's path rather than up (to windward) or down (to leeward) it. The sail is cut to carry most of its effective area higher than headsails used when the boat is working to windward.

Rhumb line The shortest distance between two points; the direct course from one mark of the course to the next.

Run To sail before the wind, or the distance sailed. Also aftermost part of the hull.

Shrouds Wire stays which support the mast laterally.

Shooting Nothing to do with firearms. A maneuver used to carry a boat to the weather side of the windward mark when to hold on would mean missing it by a few feet and having to make an extra tack to round the mark. It is executed by sharply putting the boat head to wind and using its forward momentum to *shoot* past the proper side of the buoy. It is a maneuver which requires the proper combination of favorable circumstances—good boat speed, fairly smooth water, no other boat in the way—and perfect timing. It is sometimes used at the windward finish of a very close

race in an effort to poke the bow across the line ahead of an adversary's.

Spar Term for structures on which sails are set—masts, booms, spinnaker poles.

Split tacks Racing yachts split tacks when they part company, one boat sailing on the port tack and the other on starboard.

Tacking downwind A series of jibes executed when running before light winds for the purpose of obtaining better sailing angles and thus more hull speed than would be possible by sailing the rhumb line with the breeze directly aft. The angles must be such that the increase in speed more than offsets the extra distance covered by this zig-zagging down the course.

Tender Lacking in stability; also the name for a small boat that attends a larger one.

Weather bow The bow toward which the wind is blowing. A boat is on another's *weather bow* when it is ahead on the windward side, that nearer the wind.

Weather gauge A sailing vessel has the *weather gauge* on an opponent when it is to windward of that boat.

Whistler A very strong wind, one which whistles in the rigging. Also a buoy whose sound signal is a whistle; sometimes called with very good reason a *hooter*.

Yaw To swing off course due to a following sea.